D0510633

Miss
Cranston

Miss Cranston

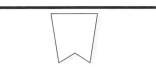

Perilla Kinchin

NMS Publishing

Published by
NMS Publishing Limited
Royal Museum, Chambers Street, Edinburgh EH1 1JF

© Perilla Kinchin 1999
Index © Helen Kemp 1999

Series editor Iseabail Macleod

*No part of this publication may be reproduced,
stored in a retrieval system or transmitted, in any
form or by any means, electronic, mechanical,
photocopying, recording or otherwise, without
the prior permission of the publisher.*

The right of Perilla Kinchin to be identified as the author of
this book has been asserted by her in accordance with the
Copyright, Designs and Patents Act 1988.

Other titles available in this series
> *Elsie Inglis*
> *The Gentle Lochiel*
> *Mungo Park*

Other books by the author include
> *Glasgow's Great Exhibitions: 1888, 1901, 1911, 1938, 1988*
> (with Juliet Kinchin & Neil Baxter)
> *Tea and Taste: The Glasgow Tea Rooms, 1875–1975*
> *Taking Tea with Mackintosh: The Story of Miss Cranston's
> Tea Rooms*

**British Library Cataloguing
in Publication Data**
A catalogue record of this book is available
from the British Library

ISBN 1 901663 13 2

Cover design by NMS Publishing Limited
Typeset by Artisan Graphics, Edinburgh
Printed in the United Kingdom by
Cambridge University Press Printing Division

ACKNOWLEDGEMENTS

It has been very difficult to find out anything very revealing or substantial about Miss Cranston — I have not turned up any letters, any scraps of her handwriting even, or any more memories. This small book is therefore based largely on research for part of my earlier study of the phenomenon of the Glasgow tea rooms. In relation to Miss Cranston I was much helped then by Dr John Mackinlay, Kate Cranston's great nephew; by the valuable interviews collected for the *Glasgow Herald* by the late Alison Downie; and by the staff of the Mitchell Library. I repeat my gratitude now. On this occasion I would also like to renew or add thanks to Douglas Annan, Neil Baxter, Helen Boullet, Elizabeth Carmichael, Alan Crawford, Margaret Hall, Jolyon Hudson, Helen Kemp, Jane Ridley and, as always, Pamela Robertson.

Illustrations

Cover: The Willow Tea Rooms in Sauchiehall Street, Glasgow. Restored to their original use, they are furnished with reproduction Charles Rennie Mackintosh. © Doug Corrance

Pages 10,43,74: T & R Annan & Sons Ltd. 24,27: Jolyon Hudson. 33: Mitchell Library, Glasgow. 36: Mitchell Library, Glasgow, photo © Hunterian Art Gallery, University of Glasgow, Mackintosh Collection. 39: George Walton Archive. 41: © Glasgow School of Art. 51: Mitchell Library, Glasgow. 54: © Alan Crawford. 58: Neil Baxter, photo Susan Scott. 62: Charles Rennie Mackintosh Society. 67: Glasgow School of Art, photo © Hunterian Art Gallery, University of Glasgow, Mackintosh Collection. 79: Glasgow Museums and Art Galleries.

Introduction

This is the story of a formidable small lady with a bright look in her eye who became one of Glasgow's best-known and best-loved characters, and whose outstanding taste and individuality enabled and supported the artistic achievements of others.

As pioneer of the famous Glasgow tearooms Miss Catherine (Kate) Cranston had a profound and beneficial effect on the social life of her native city. And as an astute and faithful patron of the 'Glasgow Style', the idiosyncratic flowering of art and design at the end of the nineteenth century, she 'deserves the art historian's unstinted gratitude', in Nikolaus Pevsner's words. Charles Rennie Mackintosh, Glasgow's great architectural hero, would have fared ill without Kate Cranston. Her name and fame now is bound up with posthumous admiration of Mackintosh, and he will feature largely in this story.

Glasgow loved Miss Cranston, and she in turn loved Glasgow, and apparently never tired of praising it. Indeed her life and business ran in parallel to the story of this great city: she was born as it found its Victorian identity in the middle of the nineteenth century, she grew to prominence as Glasgow developed towards its industrial and cultural heyday at the turn of the century.

Her retirement at the end of the First World War coincided with the end of an era for Glasgow and for Britain at large. Her last years were lived during Glasgow's spiral into decay, and she died in the depression of the thirties which was the final blow to the city's once unstoppable economy.

She was in her prime an embodiment of those qualities which produced her native city's great achievements in the last decades of the nineteenth century — with her entrepreneurial shrewdness and self-confidence, her capacity for hard work, her commitment to quality, and her adventurous interest in the new. She was 'a real business woman', and she applied the wealth she created to very pragmatic support for outstanding artistic talent. Both as a business woman and as an enlightened patron she has made a lasting contribution to Glasgow's sense of itself.

'The Glasgow man is highly individualistic', wrote that sympathetic historian of Glasgow, Charles Oakley, with the casual sexism normal at the time when he published his *Second City* in 1946. You could find no better example of this truth than Miss Cranston: that she was a Glasgow woman in a man's world was a good start.

1

George Square:
the family hotels

Catherine Cranston was born in her father's hotel in George Square, Glasgow, in 1849. When she retired from business seventy years later she returned to live in a hotel in that same square, overlooking the place where she had grown up.

The North British Railway Hotel where she took up residence was by then one of the last surviving remnants — albeit altered with an extra storey — of the dignified classical terraces which Miss Cranston had known in her youth. George Square's early mix of Georgian houses and hotels had been transformed in the interim into Glasgow's grand Victorian civic centre, a square of banks and public buildings, presided over by the ultra-opulent City Chambers.

When it was originally laid out around 1782 the square was one of Glasgow's first attempts at urban graciousness, reflecting the aspirations of the city's late eighteenth-century merchants and manufacturers, whose prosperity had superseded and broadened the tobacco- and sugar-based fortunes of the mid century, exemplifying an adaptability which was to stand Glasgow in good stead in its later history. The square had been isolated at the western edge of the town when it was first laid out, but Glasgow had spread, moving ever westward, as its population grew rapidly in the first half of the nineteenth century, along with the range and vitality of its industry and commerce: textiles, chemicals, and the beginnings of the shipbuilding and other heavy industries which would come into their

George Square before its redevelopment in the 1870s. Kate Cranston's father kept three different hotels in the square, including The Crow, *to the left of the picture. In later life Kate returned to live in the North British Railway Hotel, in the range on the right.*

own in the second half of the century. Yet as Miss Cranston recalled it for the *Glasgow Herald*, George Square in her early youth was still a largely residential area, 'what one might call the West End of Glasgow, because the residents there were doctors, lawyers, and ministers'. She remembered a gracious square with a grass park in the middle, surrounded by tall railings, to which local residents had keys. It was dotted with statues of dignitaries, and surveyed by Sir Walter Scott high in the sky on his column: this had been the first monument to be put up to him, in 1837.

Kate Cranston was born a few months before Queen Victoria's first visit to Glasgow in 1849: perhaps she was held up at the window as the royal procession passed through George Square. She was born into the world of Victoria and Albert, a Britain at mid century shaking off the last vestiges of Georgian ways and settling into a new Victorian age of progress. It was a world of possibilities, symbolised and underpinned by the newly completed railway link with London, which transformed Glasgow's place in Britain. The railway would soon carry Scots south to see the Great Exhibition of 1851, an eye-opening window on the world. Since 1842 Queen Street Station in the corner of George Square had been disgorging passengers from Edinburgh, encouraging the hotel business in the square. Meanwhile in the streets around it a new business area was growing up as the moneymakers moved west, away from the city's old business centre round Glasgow Cross and the famous Tontine Coffee House. They were leaving an area which was slipping rapidly downhill into slumdom, for here was concentrated the underside of Glasgow's industrial progress, the squalid overcrowded housing in which the poorest classes lived dazed, unhealthy and brutalised lives in the shadow of smoking factories.

Kate's father was starting his own social climb when he and his second wife moved into the Edinburgh and Glasgow Chop House and Commercial Lodgings, at number 39, on the west side of elegant George Square, not long before his daughter was born. George Cranston (1817–99), now in his early thirties, had started working life and his first family as a coachman. He had married Janet Gibson in 1839. A year later a son William was born, named after George's father; he was followed two and a half years later by Robert, named for George's grandfather. But Janet Cranston died, as did many young mothers in those days. Finding himself, still in his twenties, a widower with small children on his hands, George Cranston set about finding another wife.

On 20 November 1845 he married Grace Lace, the daughter of a joiner from Dumfriesshire. She was six or so years older than he was, so was starting married life unusually late: however she produced her first child, George, very promptly on 30 August 1846, when she was well on in her thirties. It may have been Grace who was the catalyst and practical hand behind her husband's change of profession. For he stopped being a coachman and became a 'bread, biscuit and pastry maker' at 42 Sauchiehall Street from 1846, moving the following year to number 88. Meanwhile another son, Stuart, was born early in 1848. Grace was probably already pregnant again when they took the next step upwards and moved to George Square.

George Cranston's fifth child, a daughter, arrived on 27 May 1849, and he named her Catherine, after his aunt. Catherine Cranston the elder came to live with them, and presumably made herself useful both in the family and in the business: such unmarried women, whose place in life was uncomfortable at this period, commonly attached themselves to relations as housekeepers. She could evidently have been influential upon her young namesake. Kate's mother Grace is unfortunately a shadow, and the contribution of her genes and personality to her extraordinary daughter's capacities and strong sense of herself can only be guessed. However with three children born in less than three years to attend to, and a new enterprise to build up, she must certainly have had plenty to deal with. The emotional politics of the household are closed to us, but there must have been a driving force there somewhere. As for Kate, a girl with four brothers, two of them very close in age to her, it would be a fair guess that sibling rivalry and a determination not to be disregarded were key formative factors.

Her early childhood coincided with her parents setting to work to transform what was evidently a traditional chop house and lodgings — a kind of tavern offering accommodation to commercial travellers — into something more upmarket, one of the new 'hotels'. This was reflected in its change of title to the Edinburgh and Glasgow Hotel; later it seems to have been known as the Royal Horse Hotel, or more simply 'Cranston's Hotel'. The census of 1851, giving us one of those precious ten-yearly glimpses of vanished lives, reflects this: while they have a number of tavern keepers as their neighbours in the square, George lists himself as a hotel-keeper. At this time his household consisted of himself, his wife, his children aged ten, eight, three, two and one, and his aunt Catherine, while another unmarried relative, Jessie Cranston, born in Kirkcudbright, was visiting with a companion — so 'family' numbered ten. Seven people were staying in the hotel as lodgers, including two commercial travellers from England, an engineer, a cotton-spinner, and a merchant and his wife. To look after all these there were five servants — one male and four female (two of them Irish, well exemplifying the great influx of Irish immigrants into the bottom of the heap in Glasgow in the previous decade, the 'Hungry Forties').

In abandoning the baking trade for hotel-keeping George was very probably prompted by the path his cousin Robert Cranston (1815–92) was taking. He was a year or so older than George, and born likewise at East Calder or Kirknewton outside Edinburgh, where their grandparents had settled around 1778, having moved from Jedburgh in the Borders. Robert's parents James Cranston and Janet Garvie had kept the Bay Horse Inn in East Calder before the family moved into Edinburgh in 1822. We are comparatively well-informed about this Edinburgh branch of the family as Robert Cranston rose to eminence in that city as a respected town councillor and bailie, while his son became Sir Robert and Provost. Robert Cranston was a self-made man of vigorous intelligence and personality, and he was influential on his cousin's daughter, as we shall see.

Robert had been apprenticed in the tailoring trade after he lost a leg in his teens, and the talking and reading he had done in these sedentary years had encouraged in him distinctly open-minded and indeed radical views, which reflected the general political ferment of the 1830s. It was a time when the temperance issue was beginning to be seriously discussed. Robert and two friends resolved to give up for a trial period the consumption of alcohol, a deeply ingrained part of Scottish social life at this period. Judging themselves better off without it, they took the temperance pledge.

In 1843 Robert Cranston abandoned tailoring to open with his wife Elizabeth one of the first temperance coffee houses and lodgings in Edinburgh — traditional coffee houses served plenty of ale. Its success was partly dependent on Elizabeth's renowned pies, but it was also well supplied with newspapers (which were too expensive to be taken privately by many people before duty was removed in 1861) and it became a popular meeting place for Chartists. Cranston was actively involved with this movement for political reform in the 1830s and 1840s, which seemed to the authorities to threaten revolution, and he was indeed twice briefly arrested.

Five years later, in 1848, the Cranstons sold this successful coffee house and opened the first full-blown temperance hotel, the Waverley, on Edinburgh's famed Princes Street. The choice of this prime site and the aim of making it a first-class hotel bespoke a bold conviction that it was always worth going for the best, despite the novelty of the enterprise and the doubts of observers.

Opportunistic collaboration with the new excursion tours of Thomas Cook, another Temperance supporter, led Cranston to open another Waverley Temperance Hotel in Cheapside, London in time for the Great Exhibition of 1851. The hotels became very successful and there was a move into Glasgow, with the opening of a Waverley at 185 Buchanan Street in 1860. Further expansion in Edinburgh followed. By the 1860s temperance hotels were proliferating throughout the country, and were particularly widespread in Scotland, supported by the anxiety of its middle classes about the drink problem. Cranston had pioneered what remained a very prominent feature of the Scottish social scene well into the twentieth century.

George Cranston, Kate's father, lacked his cousin's empire-building instincts, that Cranston spark and drive that was later visible in his youngest children, but he seems to have cut an effective enough figure as 'mine host', with the streak of geniality in his character which is a useful attribute for a successful hotelier. He had served in the South African wars, and was a keen peacetime soldier, joining the Queen's Own Royal Glasgow Yeomanry (first formed after rioting in the city in 1848-9) in 1855. These military connections doubtless served him well in the hotel business, and perhaps partly explain why his was not a temperance hotel. The business established itself well, and at the beginning of the 1860s George Cranston moved his family to a substantially bigger establishment, the Crow Hotel at 20 George Square, the other end of the west side of the square. The Glasgow Cranstons represent, like their Edinburgh cousins, upward mobility in action, moving steadily, through their enterprise and application, up the finely differentiated strata of the great wealth-producing middle classes which were coming into their own in these mid-Victorian years.

The next census snapshot taken on 8 April 1861 reveals that the Crow had forty windowed rooms, and that there were now nine servants: the token male to look after the boots and act as porter, and eight females, mostly in their twenties, except for one elderly unmarried pantrymaid, and including a twenty-year-old barmaid. However there were only five lodgers on this date, an auctioneer, a builder and a brewer, all from England, a draper who came from Inverness and a Glasgow-born 'warehouseman' — someone who worked in one of the furnishing and household goods stores which represented the strong growth in Glasgow's retailing at this period. The Cranston household numbered eight: we discover that George's oldest son William, who was now twenty, had become an architect and was still evidently living at home, but his brother Robert, aged eighteen, had gone, perhaps just away briefly, or maybe already seeking his fortune elsewhere. Kate was eleven, but had the company of a ten-year old cousin from Australia, George's niece Mariella Harvey, who seems to have been living with the family and going to school in Glasgow. We don't know where Kate went to school — her brother Stuart attended the Collegiate school — but she was doubtless a promising pupil. Meantime it must have been nice to have a female playmate in this house of boys. There was a visitor from Kirkcudbright too, where the Cranstons had family — seventeen-year old Mary Grier.

While Kate was growing up in the Crow, it could be said that Glasgow was growing up too. The city authorities began seriously to struggle with the dreadful problems of its too-rapid industrial growth and ever increasing population. The first major act of local government, and a great achievement, was the provision of a beautifully pure public water supply: the Loch Katrine works were opened in 1859 on another visit by Queen Victoria, who this time managed to avoid entering Glasgow itself. Despite general filth and sewerage problems, this major public work had a demonstrable positive effect on the general health of the city. In the cholera epidemic at the time of Kate's birth, in 1849–50, 3800 lives were lost; in the epidemic of 1866 only 55 died in Glasgow. Emboldened by this success and an increasing sense of civic responsibility the Town Council, which was notably forward-looking, began to take control of other aspects of the city's life. The first Medical Officer of Health was appointed in 1863, and the first attempts to grapple with slum clearance were made with the 1866 City of Glasgow Improvement Act.

Alongside this strengthening self-government developed a growing self-confidence, and there were signs that spacious George Square would become the focus of this consolidating civic identity. The square began to fill up with statues of Glasgow notables from the late 1860s. They were joined by an equestrian statue of the spirited young Queen Victoria by Baron Marochetti, which had been erected in St Vincent Place to commemorate her first visit: it was now relocated in George Square to accompany the more staid Prince Albert put up in 1866. Redevelopment of the square began right next to the Cranstons with the Italianate Bank of Scotland designed by J T Rochhead and built between 1867–70. The Crow itself was fingered for redevelopment with plans to continue this range, and at this point the family made its last move, to the Crown Hotel at number 54 in the old building adjacent to what later became the North British Railway Hotel on the north side of the square.

Not long after the move, when Kate was eighteen, her mother Grace died, on 22 October 1867. She had contracted bronchitis, which put too much strain on a weak heart. What emotional effect this death had on the family we do not know, but at the very least the loss of an active business partner must have hit George hard. Kate herself was a young woman now, old enough to think of marrying, but we might guess that, having absorbed over the years the necessary social and managerial skills, she stepped at least partly into her mother's shoes, supplying the hotel's feminine touch.

During the years of her growth to adulthood Kate had been able to look to Robert Cranston's outstandingly capable wife Elizabeth as a role model, and perhaps now she found in her a substitute mother figure. From 1860 Mrs Cranston had spent much time in Glasgow — she apparently was solely responsible for running the Glasgow Waverley on Buchanan Street, so presumably lived separately from her husband for long periods. The daughter of a Leith carter, Elizabeth Dalgliesh was remembered in the family biography as 'a large-hearted woman, remarkably able and phenomenally rapid and accurate with figures'. Her son Sir Robert Cranston paid tribute with love and admiration to her role in running the business: 'the success of the hotels was principally due to my mother. There never was a better mother and a more loyal woman. From morning till midnight she was at her post, whilst my father, although managing the general affairs, was given more to politics and the people than to his business.'

Robert Cranston had been indeed from his young days politically aware, and during the 1860s he was becoming increasingly well-connected and involved in local politics: he was on the Edinburgh Town Council from 1868 and later became a highly respected bailie. He had progressive views on women, and was an early suffragist supporter, having learnt a deep respect for women's talents from his own family — his paternal grandmother, a strong personality; his well-educated mother; and of course his wife. He spent freely on the education of his daughters. In his oldest daughter Mary he recognised another born business woman; he wanted her to use her talents, not surrender them to upper middle-class social convention, as was evident from his wedding present to her when she married the Glasgow photographic dealer George Mason in 1872. It was nothing less than a hotel — the Washington Temperance Hotel on Sauchiehall Street (later renamed the Waverley Temperance Hotel when the original Waverley was sold in 1885). Mary was about three years older than her cousin Kate and the two developed a lifelong friendship.

So with the example of her Edinburgh cousins before her Kate could see that women could handle business as well as any man, and could fulfil themselves in doing so. She must have learnt naturally from them and from her parents' hotel that quality of service, attention to detail and new ideas meant good business. It was reputation that built customer loyalty and kept people coming back.

Among the valued regulars of George Cranston's hotels — first at the Crow, then at the Crown — was one who was early on a crucial link in the development of the tearoom story. This was the portly and characterful gentleman who represented the London tea firm of Twining's, Arthur Dakin, 'more like a bishop than a bagman'. He clearly wove a tale of romance and possibilities round tea: Glasgow's importing commerce was burgeoning at this period, and it was a significant rival to London in the tea trade. He fixed up Kate's brother Stuart, as a teenager fresh from school and susceptible to the glamour of expertise, with a post as invoice clerk with the tea dealers Wright, Napier & Co.

Stuart began by doing his stint in the freezing despatch warehouse but soon managed to find his way into the warmth of the tea-tasting room, where he was taken under the wing of James Williamson. This expert taster was evidently won by the Cranston eagerness to excel, and began the slow process of training the young man's palate. Later after a disastrous fortnight as a sales rep for another firm Stuart Cranston crept back to work under his old mentor as a sub-agent for Tetley & Co, continuing to apply himself with keen determination to the slow accumulation of experience which makes a fine tea merchant.

In 1871, at the age of only twenty-three, Stuart boldly set up by himself at 44 St Enoch Square as a retailer of tea, and when we get our next glimpse of the Cranstons in the census of that year we find him listing himself proudly as a tea merchant. His brother George was also pursuing expertise as a chemist in the chemical industry, another significant branch of the city's industrial make-up, but at the time of the census he was apparently living elsewhere. In fact the household in the Crown had shrunk at the time of this official count to only father George, Stuart and Kate. There were nine lodgers, including a liquor dealer and his wife, and a distiller (proof again that no temperance rule applied in this Cranston hotel), an English landowner and a flour and grain merchant, and interestingly a Glasgow-born landscape painter. Two young male servants in addition to eight females shows a slight increase in the number of retainers over the tally at the Crow ten years before.

The death of Elizabeth Cranston at the Glasgow Waverley Hotel in 1873 was doubtless a sharp loss for Kate. As the 1870s edged on her world was changing in many ways. Glasgow was entering upon a new era of industrial and commercial maturity. Its heavy industries, marine engineering and steel-making were growing with matchless confidence: by 1876 Glasgow was building one third of all British tonnage. The Clyde was being progressively deepened and docks built; commerce was expanding multifariously. A variety of manufacturing enterprises spawned by the fitting out of ships and locomotives was supplying the city with the highest levels of craft skill.

Central Glasgow was being heavily rebuilt as Glasgow sought to express this Victorian industrial maturity in stone, asserting its status as Second City of Empire, and George Square was undergoing a particularly thorough transformation. On the west side, the old Crow finally disappeared in 1874 under the extension to the Bank of Scotland range by one of Glasgow's leading architects James Sellars, while John Burnet's opulent Merchant's House of 1874–7 flattened George Cranston's first hotel: this was a replacement for the seventeenth-century Merchant's Hall demolished some time since in Bridgegate. Glasgow was determinedly sweeping away its small-town past and giving itself a new urban face. The fine old seventeenth-century university buildings on the old High Street which had likewise been engulfed by slums had been recently replaced by new Gothic buildings on Gilmorehill in the salubrious West of Glasgow: there had been a high holiday in 1868 when the Prince and Princess of Wales laid the ceremonial foundation stone for the new building. The Princess was back in 1876 to do the same for the grand new Post Office on the south side of George Square. The transformation of the square was to be completed in the 1880s by the enormous City Chambers on the east side.

The Crown was now one of the last remaining hotels in what had been a Georgian square of small chop houses, boarding houses, businesses and homes when the Cranstons came. George was interesting himself in his son's growing tea business, and, perhaps disliking the new environment or finding the hotel business intractable without his wife, he decided to retire from it, though he was only in his mid fifties. None of his sons was interested in the hotel business, and it seems that Kate did not want to stay in it either, or did not count. So some time around 1874 the family abandoned George Square and moved to a tenement flat at 91 Sauchiehall Street, opposite where George had been in business all those years ago at number 88, and just along from Mary Mason in her hotel at 172 (the site now occupied by Marks & Spencer).

In 1875 Stuart Cranston moved his expanding tea business to new premises at 76 Argyle Street, on the corner with Queen Street, ideally situated near commercial premises, shops and restaurants. And here it was that a new era in the Cranston story began and the tearooms were born.

2

'A cup of Kaisow 2d. Bread and cakes extra': the birth of the tearooms

Stuart Cranston, in whose character one senses a touch of monomania, was almost fanatical on the subject of tea. He was a passionate China-tea man himself: in later decades this meant a hopeless crusade against the increasing popularity of Indian and Ceylon tea sold in packets by such as his contemporary, Glasgow's great grocery entrepreneur, Thomas Lipton. In the 1870s, however, while tea drinking was strongly on the increase, China tea was still the dominant taste. Ever keen to educate his customers on the qualities of his different leaves, Cranston customarily kept a kettle at hand to offer tastings. Hitting upon the innovative idea of charging for this, and supplying some simple bakery to go with it — who knows, it may even have been his sister's suggestion — he set aside space for twelve customers to sit 'elbow to elbow' and advertised 'A cup of Kaisow 2d. Bread and cakes extra'. Thus came into existence the first tearoom — the first tearoom anywhere, it was alleged. Glasgow was used to inventing things and was quite happy for Stuart, apparently rightly, to claim this: it was eight years, it seems, before there was any such place in London. After a slowish start the word spread, and the tearoom became well used, especially by ladies.

That it was an extension of shopping for tea made it safe and attractive for women. Middle-class women, who had been penned at home for decades by Victorian ideas about angels of the hearth and so on, were becoming keen to get out, and shopping was increasingly seen as a passport to some sort of freedom and choice. At the same time it had not developed yet, as it would in the next decades, into a fully-blown leisure activity, and while Glasgow already had some fine shops, and retailing was expanding strongly, there was a dearth of facilities in the centre of town which women could use. It was still very difficult for females to go anywhere unaccompanied — the places that men used for refreshment were out of the question. The tearoom also hit the spot with men, simply by appearing at a time when the economy was booming: there were ample opportunities for anyone able to exploit the gap between supply and demand for convenient light refreshments. There was a need here that Stuart Cranston had stumbled upon, though for the time being he concentrated on building up his business and reputation as a tea dealer.

Kate was clearly watching with keen interest. For one thing she was not properly employed now that the family hotel had gone — though it may be that she was actively helping Stuart. In conventional terms of course, with a widowed father and two unmarried brothers to look after, her life was quite adequately and dutifully filled; her only anxiety should have been the search for a husband, for now in her late twenties she was clearly already 'on the shelf' in most people's books.

Why was she not married indeed? She was attractive and vivacious and intelligent, with a lively sense of humour. One can see that her evident lack of submissiveness must have put a lot of men off; but she was not without suitors, it seems. However she evidently did not want the respectably restricted life which marriage offered an upwardly mobile middle-class woman. She had management in her bones. She wanted independence, the opportunity to do things the way she wanted. A different woman might have moved from her father's business into her brother's: Glasgow's business world was full of women hidden by men in this way, but contributing very significantly to the flourishing economy. Kate Cranston's clear wish to go it alone is symptomatic of her individuality. Cooperation — or Kate's subordination — in a joint enterprise with her brother would have been difficult, we sense, for two strong characters.

In her belief that she could break through the normal hindrance of being female Kate had invaluable encouragement from her own relations — from the Waverley Cranstons that is. There is a family tradition that George opposed her ambitions: this may not be true — but it is possible that he felt personally threatened by her wish to do more than give him and his sons a comfortable home. Perhaps there was also a feeling that she should have been devoting herself to her brother George, who was probably already showing signs of the tuberculosis that was to kill him. Stuart might not have been able to stifle feelings of sibling jealousy. We don't know. Whatever the truth, it seems that practical help, the money to start up, came from Kate's father's cousin, Robert Cranston, in Edinburgh, while moral support from his wife and his daughter Mary was on the doorstep in Glasgow. It looks as if these connections found her premises on the street floor of Robert Cranston's friend John Aitken's Temperance Hotel at 114 Argyle Street.

So with backing from her well-established cousins, with plenty of her own experience of the family hotel business behind her, and the example of her brother's pioneering 'tearoom' before her, Kate Cranston set off on her own career. Family tradition has it that she paid leave-taking calls on her friends 'because she said she knew that they would not want to know her when she had become a business woman'. In 1878 she opened up her Crown Tea and Luncheon Rooms, named after the now defunct family hotel.

Her listing as plain 'C. Cranston' in the Glasgow Post Office Directory looks like a deliberate attempt to disguise her sex for business purposes. It also neatly defeated the invidious pecking order of the listings, which, reflecting social realities, put men of any particular surname first, then married women and finally unmarried women. By her subterfuge she appeared in the list near the top and above her brother, a small but satisfying victory. She described herself as a restaurateur, and from the beginning she catered on a much more serious basis than Stuart, providing lunches and substantial high teas, as well as coffees and afternoon teas. She was thus the real pioneer of the typical Glasgow tearoom of later decades, and was indeed the first to use the term 'tearoom' in the directories, while Stuart, who defined himself very intently as a tea merchant, still referred to his 'sample room', seeing it as an entrepreneurial side shoot of his serious dry-tea retailing business.

In the concept she had, as well as in the location she chose on Glasgow's lively everyday business street, Kate Cranston had clearly identified the particular needs of business men. Men were working harder these days, and had been also moving their families out of the smoky city centre to the new residential suburbs, so that the old habit of going home for dinner in the middle of the day was disappearing. The tramway system initiated in 1872 and expanding at the end of the decade was a crucial step in this development, enabling people to run conveniently in and out of town. Men were now looking for 'lunch' to quell rumbling stomachs, as it became the fashion to eat the day's main meal in the early evening. Alongside restaurants this demand sprouted innovative responses like Lang's in Queen Street, already going strong in the 1860s, serving famously numerous varieties of sandwich, washed down with milk, whisky or ale, all eaten on the hoof, on a help-yourself system (p. 24). At the same time there was an old male habit of meeting under the pretext of 'business' for a 'meridian' — a drink and a smoke late-morning — or again at the end of work. This was catered for by pubs and taverns, or businesses like pie shops or pastry bakers (George Cranston had probably run such a place back in the 1840s), or by coffee rooms.

All these places were distinctly male in orientation, and most of them quite out of the question for an unaccompanied female. For women, as we have already seen, somewhere in the city centre where they could respectably go, alone if need be, to sit down and rest their weary feet, have a little refreshment and sociable converse and use 'conveniences' was desperately needed. Men were well provided for, women quite the reverse. It's easy to see how the Cranstons' enterprises were a godsend to women, but why were they so successful with men?

A key element here was the temperance movement, which we have already encountered as the basis of the Edinburgh 'Waverley' Cranstons' growing prosperity. Robert Cranston was prominent in the temperance cause through his high-profile hotels with their inflexible no-alcohol rule, and though George Cranston had not run a dry establishment the family influence was strong on the next generation. Both Kate and Stuart were abstainers — practical if not full-blown subscribed ones.

In general the pressure against alcohol would not go away, and it was particularly strong in Glasgow, whose reputation as Britain's most drink-sodden city flourished alongside its achievements as the Workshop of the World. Though admonition and interference were directed mainly at the working classes, it was middle-class women, who often had private experience of alcoholic fathers and husbands, who exercised a lot of influence in the movement. By the late 1870s the old male business-social life was coming under severe pressure. Many a man must have felt it worth

Lang's in 1881, no. 1 in Quiz *magazine's 'Sights of the City' series. A quick lunch for businessmen, but not alcohol free.*

buying a quiet life at home by being able to say hand on heart that he had gone to Miss Cranston's for his lunch, rather than to the Pope's Eye Tavern, or Sloan's. Respectability was to become a hugely profitable asset for the tearooms as temperance sentiment took a firm hold of everyday life.

Kate Cranston had the protective mantle of a temperance hotel above her (Argyle Street had some reputation for drunken rowdiness in the evening) but she was not pushing temperance down her customers' throats. Businessmen could meet for their smoke over a quickly served coffee, or for their cheap and well-cooked lunch in pleasing surroundings. Miss Cranston was in effect supporting that more sympathetic branch of the temperance movement which proposed to wean men from drink with attractive alternatives, rather than the faction that wished to impose prohibition. Her establishment did not have the dourness of temperance coffee houses: it was something pleasant and new, acceptable to womenfolk as well as their husbands.

The coffee habit became ingrained in Glasgow's business life, and was connected with a general decline in drunkenness. There was no doubt that Kate had hit upon something for which there was a demand. It was hard work getting the business going all the same.

Since they had left George Square in the mid 1870s Kate and her father and brothers had been living at 91 Sauchiehall Street and that is where they still were when the census came round again on 4 April 1881. It was a tenement flat with five windowed rooms — not a great amount of space for five adults (including their live-in servant Mary Wilson, who would have slept in the traditional set-in bed in the kitchen); but lavish indeed given the current statistics on overcrowding in Glasgow overall. Dr J B Russell, the city's current Medical Officer of Health, a humane and eloquent man who was struggling to draw attention to the appallingly overcrowded housing conditions of the poor at this period, pointed out in 1881 that only five per cent of Glasgow's housing stock had five or more rooms; thirty per cent of houses were of one room only, and that space often shared by several inhabitants. To have a bedroom of one's own that was not also used by the family was a luxury that even the prosperous middle classes did not expect.

Glasgow was still moving inexorably west as the residential areas of the West End developed as the new place to live. Sauchiehall Street, which had been a mix of housing and small businesses, was slowly beginning to be redeveloped at the eastern end as a commercial street. Copland & Lye, drapers, established themselves there from 1878, to be followed in the next decade by other 'warehouses': these were the forerunners of the full-blown department stores of the end of the century. Later in 1881 the Cranstons moved west themselves along Sauchiehall Street, reflecting this shift in Glasgow's urban nature and their own growing prosperity, to number 425, near Charing Cross.

This was a bigger flat, with seven as opposed to five main rooms, allowing for the niceties of upper middle-class living with a separate drawing room and dining room, as well as dedicated sleeping rooms. It was soon very spacious, as Stuart left home when he married Flora MacLachlan in January 1882 and moved out to the newly fashionable suburb of Bearsden. Interestingly the flat appears in the directories under Kate's name: it seems that her brother George had left home too — though he was there with his family two years later when he died of tuberculosis, at the age of thirty-eight, on 28 October 1884.

During these years Kate certainly had plenty on her plate. Things had been difficult for a little after the crash of the City of Glasgow Bank in October of the year of Kate's opening, 1878. This devastated the city's commercial life, but the forward movement behind its industrial and commercial growth was evident in the rapidity with which the economy picked up again. By the middle of the 1880s things were booming once more, and both Cranstons were ready to expand their businesses. Stuart, now more mindful of the commercial possibilities of the tearooms, and especially of female custom, at last expanded his cramped table space with new tearooms higher up Queen Street, advertising in addition to 'The first tea rooms in the city' at 2 Queen Street, 'Superior Accommodation for Ladies at our Branch Tea Rooms, No. 46 Queen Street'. 'At Both Establishments Ladies Shopping, and Gentlemen during Business Hours, may obtain "A cup of Mandarin Tea for 2d., with Cream and Sugar," Served Instantly. Bread, Biscuits, Etc., extra.'

Kate took on new premises at 205 Ingram Street, opened on 16 September 1886. These were well placed in Glasgow's commercial area, aiming chiefly at business men, though again ladies were not forgotten. The *Bailie* magazine, beginning an approval of Miss Cranston that was to continue over many years, gave her a little write-up which secured to her some of the tea expertise that Stuart always claimed:

> That lady, who is the originator of the cup of tea business in a tea shop… is as great an authority on the qualities of tea as she is skilled in the best mode of preparing it; and gracious in manner, and of a thorough business capacity, her tables ought to be well frequented.

It comments in particular on the comfortable arrangements, picking up their identifiably feminine character:

> There is a large commodious room for gentlemen, and a neat little apartment — I should almost say arbour — for ladies. The painting of the walls and ceilings is of the most artistic charm, and is altogether in the style of the "flowery land".

A fuzzy photograph survives to show a decorative scheme in 'artistic' taste, with touches of the fashionable japonisme alluded to by the *Bailie*, and some of the stained leaded glass in which Glasgow was developing a strong tradition at this period. The style of the whole thing is broadly influenced by the Aesthetic Movement and its guru Whistler, who had

An advertisement in 'artistic' graphic style for 'C. Cranston's' new Ingram Street
premises, opened in 1886.

many adherents among Glasgow's artistic set at this period. A smoking room, further specialised provision for men, was opened a little later.

An advertisement for the new rooms shows Kate still hiding behind 'C. Cranston'. And it reveals some kind of business input from her brother: perhaps it was after all an attempt at a cooperative business venture. Indeed these premises were confusingly listed as 'Cranston's Tea Rooms' in the street directory and they appeared under Stuart's name — to Kate's disgust? — in Baddeley's guide issued in 1888. This raises again the tantalising question of Kate's relationship with her brother. In family tradition they were 'great friends'. A popular belief that they hated each other is probably an extrapolation of what clearly became a keen business rivalry. However there are signs later that they preferred to keep a certain distance from each other, and whatever the situation in 1886 we can see how 'taste' was becoming a way in which Kate clearly differentiated herself and her tearooms from the other Cranston rooms.

Despite the focus on men as customers, the advertisement for the new tearooms evokes something distinctly feminine. It is in the same broadly 'artistic' taste as the tearoom interiors. This was a period of great interest in the decoration of the home, which was regarded as a key arena for the display of feminine values. The 1880s saw a flood of manuals which set out to instruct women who were desperate to know how to create the requisite havens of taste — how to protect their homes and families with beauty and art from the dirty, ugly world of work outside. Kate Cranston was offering something similar in the heart of the city centre, an escape from commercial values into tasteful domesticity. This was to be the key to the way she developed her business identity, and it was to lead her out from behind 'C. Cranston' to parade her feminine identity — Miss Cranston was about to emerge into full view.

Making a name: Miss Cranston's Tea Rooms

In the 1880s Glasgow was really hitting its stride, building on the progress of the 1870s, looking forward with confidence. The first telephone appeared in 1879 and the system expanded rapidly in the business centre in the following decade. Handsome buildings rose up in the city centre, like the massive Central Station Hotel opened in 1884 to trump the Glasgow and South-Western Railway's St Enoch Station Hotel, and embodying the success of the Caledonian railway company. Back in George Square the foundation stone was laid in 1883 for the mighty bulk of the City Chambers, planned on a suitably grandiose scale: Queen Victoria was booked to open them in state in 1888. This city of merchants and industrialists, self-made and entrepreneurial, was ready now to assert its civic and cultural identity with some significant gesture.

To lay claim to its status as Second City of Empire and to celebrate this new confidence Glasgow decided to stage its first International Exhibition of Art and Industry. 1888 was to be a big year for the city, and proved to be indeed the beginning of its golden age. Glasgow was entering the world arena alongside other great capitalist manufacturing centres which had staged such shows ever since Prince Albert's Great Exhibition got it all going in London in 1851. The most immediate aim was to trounce the exhibitions held by Glasgow's old adversary Edinburgh in 1886, and its major industrial competitor Manchester in 1887.

The opening of exhibition year brought a flurry of sprucing up for the anticipated floods of visitors — roads were remade, shop fronts repainted, tramway attendants kitted out in new uniforms. There was a sense of mounting excitement as the enormous domed main building of painted and gilded wood went up in Kelvingrove Park, surrounded by picturesque minor structures — all vaguely oriental in effect, so that the show was soon dubbed 'Baghdad by the Kelvin'. With buildings that had only to last out a summer's rain the exhibition was a chance to go for effect and a touch of novelty and exoticism. The financing and general preparations were carried out with an efficiency befitting Glasgow's corporate business acumen, and the last-minute chaos which frequently attended such ambitious events was largely avoided.

Kate Cranston was affected by this mood of experimentation and the whiffs of a new style for the end of the century that were now circulating. Her early tearooms in Argyle Street, to judge from a dim old photograph, had evoked comfortable domestic surroundings: we glimpse plush chairs and even antlers on the wall. The decor at Ingram Street, where she employed established firms of decorators, had been in good but not extraordinary 'artistic' taste. But to freshen up parts of her Argyle Street premises, now ten years old, for exhibition year she made an impulsive gesture towards something a bit different and new. She employed a young man from an artistic family who had been working, rather miserably, as a bank clerk and doing odd decorating jobs for the circle of his acquaintance — George Walton. He was a younger brother of Edward (E A) Walton, one of the 'Glasgow Boys', a loose group of young men painting in a fresh impressionist style who were emerging to prominence at this period. Edward was currently engaged along with his friends James Guthrie, George Henry and John Lavery in painting decorations in the dome of the main Exhibition building, while others executed murals in the Fine Art section. This progressive public patronage was perhaps prompted by willingness to endorse the obvious revolt of these young men against the stuffy academic establishment of Edinburgh. John Lavery was commissioned to paint the state visit of Queen Victoria later in the year, and several of the Boys later added their contributions to the opulent mishmash of decorations in the City Chambers.

George Walton, a reserved yet very versatile and creative young man, grasped the opportunity Miss Cranston gave him with both hands. A small photograph of a corner of the redecorated Argyle Street tearoom gives a glimpse of the distinctively refined and elegant stencilled rose and briar pattern he used. It attests the influence of both Whistler and Morris on their young devotee, an influence combined and absorbed into something innovative and fresh. Walton brought to his decorating work a highly developed sense of colour harmonies.

It was the beginning of Kate Cranston's career as a patron of the 'new art', and a truly discriminating act — it was probably on the strength of this commission, his first real professional job, that the twenty-year-old Walton in 1888 threw up banking and set up a small business as 'George Walton & Co, Ecclesiastical and House Decorators'. Looking back from 1906 in an article in the influential *Studio* art magazine, J Taylor opined: 'It is not easy to imagine what would be the position of modern decorative art in Glasgow to-day, apart from the group of tea-houses controlled by Miss Cranston'; for with George Walton's abandonment of finance 'decorative art may be said to have entered on the new phase at Glasgow.' In his approach to the integrated interior Walton was the pioneer of what has become known as the Glasgow Style, which developed in the next decade to reach its height by the time of Glasgow's next great exhibition in 1901.

The 1888 exhibition, an overwhelming display of 'Art and Industry', had as its stated aim the funding of a new Art Gallery, Museum and Art School. An interest in high art was a proper aspiration of any mature world city, but in Glasgow there was developing a powerful and relevant appreciation of the importance of design in connection with progressive industry, and this more practical conviction was behind the drive to develop new connections between the art school and industry. Glasgow's high level of craft and manufacturing skills in interior decoration were already well in evidence at the exhibition — this was a strength deriving from the established tradition of ship and locomotive fitting. Combined with the city's characteristic openness to the new, it gave a good platform for the development of a distinctive achievement in design. Kate Cranston was in there at the beginning, and would be there at the end, three decades later.

How she met George Walton we do not know, but she was well placed to get to know interesting people and doubtless had plenty of customers from Glasgow's art world. The Waltons, though now somewhat im-poverished, were well connected in the upper echelons of middle-class

Glasgow life. 'Lively and original' herself, Kate seems to have collected a number of younger male admirers in the artistic set. One of these was James Craig Annan (1864–1946), a rising star in the late 1880s, becoming known for his 'artistic' photography. He was a friend of Walton's, whose new decorating company's premises at 152 Wellington Street were adjacent to T & R Annan's goods entrance.

Fifty years later on the eve of the 1938 Empire Exhibition the elderly Annan looked out for *The Scottish Field* six photographs of Glasgow leading lights. He included a portrait of Miss Cranston of which he was particularly proud, and the affection of his memory is clear, as is that sympathy with the subject which is essential for a good portrait. She looks straight out of the picture, bright and lively in one of her favourite feathered hats and a ruched jacket of mid-Victorian appearance. Her style of dress is something we shall come back to. Another shot taken at the same sitting shows her in profile, plump but neatly upholstered and erect. It is hard to tell how old she is — she would have turned thirty-nine shortly after the 1888 exhibition opened, while Annan would have been around twenty-four.

Glasgow was deeply smitten by its first exhibition. It was the first time, in the words of Neil Munro (1864–1930) — another of Miss Cranston's young admirers — that Glasgow 'let itself go'. Here was an intoxicating illuminated world, 'where the sun shines all day and the electric all night'. The abnormally wonderful weather, the rich diversity of exhibits, the gondolas on the Kelvin, the new and soon beloved switchback — all offered an escape from drab reality. The pleasures of taking tea, in surroundings enhanced by fancy dress and colourful architecture, were one of the exhibition's discoveries. The India and Ceylon Tea Rooms had service by fascinatingly exotic orientals; or there was a Dutch cocoa house; or Assafrey's elegant tearoom above its confectionery kiosk. The Bishop's Palace Temperance Café run by Jo Lyons with tea supplied by Cooper's, a Glasgow tea firm founded in the same year as Stuart Cranston's, had ranks of waitresses in Mary Queen of Scots rig — Lyons' widows, they were called. (Joseph Lyons opened his famous chain of tea shops in London a few years later, having perhaps observed the Cranstons' success in Glasgow.) Meanwhile the Glasgow School of Cookery tearoom in the Women's Art and Industries section was one of several efforts in this section to promote the possibilities of gainful employment for middle-class women.

The early portrait of Kate Cranston selected by the well-known photographer James Craig Annan looking through his album of Glasgow personalities in 1938, roughly half a century after it was taken.

City-centre businesses worked flat out to capitalise on the huge influx of visitors to Glasgow (attendance at the exhibition hit 5.75 million), and there was a sudden feeling of cosmopolitanism abroad. Kate Cranston must have been as swept up as anyone by the great show and the commercial opportunities it offered. Next time she would be in the thick of it.

Meanwhile in the expansive spirit encouraged by the exhibition she seized the chance to acquire the lease of the ground floor at 209 Ingram

Street next to her tearooms at 205, and in August quickly announced (now calling herself Miss Cranston, we note) the impending opening of new luncheon rooms. These were prepared at breakneck speed in an attempt to open in September, before all the extra exhibition custom was lost, but she must have wished that the chance had come up earlier. For this job she employed William Scott Morton, a Glaswegian whose recently established Edinburgh-based decorating firm had developed the embossed canvas wall covering Tynecastle Canvas which was currently all the rage: it was showcased at the exhibition in the Bishop's Castle, and was used in the decoration of the City Chambers. The decoration of Miss Cranston's new space was apparently in this slightly heavy 'artistic' taste, but in keeping with the ethos of the exhibition she advertised 'Electric Light Used Throughout'.

The after-effects of the exhibition could be felt in a new self-confidence in Glasgow's material and cultural life, a greater sophistication and interest in enjoyment. It propelled Glasgow into the nineties, a period of newness, no longer 'Victorian' except in so far as the aging Queen still ruled. There was a great increase in tea drinking, and new tearooms began to open thick and fast.

Stuart Cranston, having now fully grasped the possibilities of tearooms in parallel to his dry tea business, led the way by opening a major new enterprise at 26 Buchanan Street in 1889, the biggest set of tearooms in Britain. This made the occasion for the coveted *Bailie* 'Men You Know' profile which began 'The tea room is among the newer features of Glasgow life' and went on to pinpoint the 'felt need' which the tearoom had so effectively filled. 'Neither a public house nor a pastry cooks', it has a character of its own, and one which commends itself to the community generally'. The *Bailie*, which represented a core of stout resistance in Glasgow society to hard-line temperance, could see that the service provided by the tearooms appealed on its own merits, without any browbeating: 'Mr Cranston has done more, probably, to advance the cause of temperance, than all the Permissive Bill agitators put together'. (These were people lobbying for the power to effect total prohibition locally.)

The large hall-like main tearoom at Buchanan Street, with its rows of tables and plush banquettes set out in the refectory style then common in restaurants, emphasises by contrast the feminine domestic quality that his sister was bringing to the tearooms. Cranston bent what the *Bailie* nicely describes as his 'eager, fervid nature' upon features like a new ventilation system of which he was extremely proud. By 1889 Cranston's Tea Rooms Ltd and Miss Cranston's Tea Rooms were clearly separated, though confusion about the sibling businesses always persisted in some quarters. But a gap in taste is there to be seen: 'Miss' and 'artistic taste' were the keys to Kate's business identity.

The 1890s was a decade of great growth: new offices and new shops sprang up in the city centre. It was a decade of the new indeed: the 'new art' — Beardsley, Wilde, Whistler, as well as Glasgow's own 'spook school' — scandalised conventional society; and the 'new woman' was making waves (1892 was significant as the year in which Glasgow University agreed to offer degrees to women). There was a general sense of change in society. Daily life was being generally transformed: in 1891 the first municipal electricity generating station was opened, and two years later electric street lighting began to appear. With its growing zeal for running services the Corporation took over the trams in 1894 and made them by the end of the century, when electrification began, a hugely effective mass transport system. Another exciting event was the opening of the underground railway or subway in 1896, though it had teething problems. Telephones were now widely established, while towards the end of the decade the motor-car, that other harbinger of the twentieth century, began to be seen on the streets. Moving films, first shown in Glasgow in 1896, caught on rapidly, and 'Kodak-fiends' pursued the new fad of amateur snapping.

Stuart Cranston drove on with his tearooms — he opened another at 43 Argyll Arcade in 1892, and then went on to buy the whole of the arcade block from what he would insist on calling Argyll Street (Argyle Street to others, but he had a bee in his bonnet about the 'correct' spelling) to Buchanan Street. Property investment in Glasgow's developing city centre became a cornerstone of his company.

As for Miss Cranston, she marked this era of the new woman by suddenly and surprisingly, at the advanced age of 43, getting married. On 7 July 1892 she wed John Cochrane according to the forms of the United Presbyterian Church at the Windsor Hotel on St Vincent Street. He was the eldest son of the founder of the Grahamston Foundry and Boiler Works in Barrhead, south of Glasgow.

Marriage at this period should have meant the end of Miss Cranston: that is to say that powerful social conventions decreed that women should

John Cochrane, who had his own distinctive style of dress. He was eight years younger than Kate Cranston, whom he married in 1892.

give up paid employment on marriage to devote themselves to the important task of home-making, giving their husband the role of head of house and provider. But it was not the end: in lots of ways, as we shall see, it was just the beginning. A sign of her refusal to give way in her independent ambitions was her retention of her maiden name, which was now a notable business name, at work, though she was just as firmly 'Mrs Cochrane' at home. For a woman to marry for the first time in her forties was very unusual. But of course Kate Cranston was nothing if not unusual.

In John Cochrane, about eight years younger than her, she found someone who appreciated her strength and eccentricity, indeed adored her for it. He was a mild man, artistically disposed: he had his own line in idiosyncratic dress, affecting tall stove-pipe hats and dashing capes. He was later recalled as 'a flamboyant artistic type of man who all his days was dominated by women', first his mother, then his wife. He must have been willing to be bossed around, for Kate was certainly used to getting her own way. But the relationship worked: they are remembered as a most devoted couple.

Kate moved with her new husband to East Park, a spacious semi-detached house on the Carlibar Road in Barrhead, taking with her the elderly and dependent George Cranston. As an omen of what was to come Kate chose to transform the interiors of her first married home with a touch of the 'new art', calling back in 1893–4 the young designer whose career she had pretty much launched in 1888. George Walton had been busy in the intervening years, working in and around Glasgow's artistic set, developing his innovative ideas. At East Park he applied the range of skills that his small firm could now offer, producing for the job furniture, including a painted piano; stained glass; stencilled decoration; and some elegant woodwork, including fitted seating, in the drawing room. An ogee arch and fretted trellis lent a touch of the orientally fanciful which had proved so bewitching at the recent exhibition. The colour schemes are lost now, but it was in this area that George's painterly eye came to the fore. Kate must have been pleased with the work.

Marriage gave her new strength. Cochrane was well-off: the boiler-making business established by his father in 1850, which he now ran with his two brothers Archibald and William, was reaching its peak at this period, its history of growth representative of many such businesses in Glasgow and its environs. He had the practicality of a mechanical engineer and good financial experience: from the business as well as the personal point of view Kate had made a good marriage. She now had capital behind her, and her husband supported her ambitions (at the cost it was said of his family business, which declined in the new century — but there were deeper underlying economic reasons for this). The story of the next years is of investment in extending the tearooms. All Kate's dealings were in her own name, 'Catherine Cranston or Cochrane', though as legally necessary with the consent of her husband.

Life for Kate settled into a pattern of daily commuting into Glasgow on the trains, along with thousands of others who worked in the city but lived at its edges. The couple had a busy social life in Barrhead and Glasgow. They were fond of music, and fond of children. John Cochrane, marrying in his thirties, might have hoped to be a father, but Kate's age was against her, even if she had wished it. They found surrogate family in her cousin Mary Mason's children, a boy and four girls, the youngest of whom, Elliot, was born in 1888, exhibition year, and in the daughters of John's favourite brother Archibald, Isabel and Jean, to whom they were also close. Their businesses and participation in the rich fabric of civic life around them kept them well occupied. Kate in particular was preparing something big.

Her brother Stuart had made his headquarters in his large premises in Buchanan Street, down at the Argyle Street end. Now Kate too was planning something that would put her well on the map, a move into this premier shopping street, higher up among prestigious shops. Having established her premises on Argyle Street and Ingram Street firmly in the daily routines of business people she was now more obviously aiming at a leisured female clientele as well. Though not really very far from her other establishments this was a different proposition altogether: Buchanan Street had been Glasgow's street of quality from its beginnings, and still maintained its class.

In May 1894 Miss Cranston acquired 91–3 Buchanan Street, the Alexandra Café, which had been in business as long as Miss Cranston herself, from 1878. This was an expensive property, valued at £5000 in 1895 when application was made to take down the old building, and put up another. Whether Kate had originally intended to take over the earlier building but then found it unworkable for some reason is not known; however a general enthusiasm for rebuilding was obstructing much of

The builder's barricade, imaginatively decorated by the young George Walton, in front of the new Buchanan Street tearooms, opened in 1897.

central Glasgow in this decade. At all events it was a long job. Work started in June 1895 and took two full years. To pay for the rebuilding she raised the then enormous sum of £14000 as a mortgage on the property from John George Stewart, a carpet manufacturer.

She was evidently determined to do this properly. Miss Cranston was going to make her mark.

4

New art 'weirdry': Miss Cranston and the Glasgow Style

Miss Cranston planned a full suite of assorted tea and luncheon rooms, with segregated provision for ladies if they wished it, and smoking and billiard rooms as havens for the men, in a brand new building on four floors with the kitchen in the basement. She turned to an Edinburgh architect: George Washington Browne, who did a lot of banks. He produced a well-made, quite ornate 'artistic' façade in a revivalist style, very suitable for its upmarket location. However Kate brought in George Walton, whom she now regarded as 'her interior designer', to handle the decoration and furnishing. Work started on fitting up the interior in November 1896.

An early sign of what was going to emerge was characteristically unorthodox: the builder's barricade (p. 39) was stencilled by Walton with a flowing Whistlerian peacock and new graphic touches which announced the stylishness of 'Miss Cranston's New Lunch & Tea Rooms' well in advance. There is no record of any earlier hoarding having been treated like this. Walton had transformed something ordinary into something different and special by the application of art — just as was happening within. It was a brilliant advertisement.

Walton must have wished he had a similarly plain surface to work boldly but simply upon inside, but there were quite a lot of intrusive ornamental touches — ornate woodwork, fancy panelling, fireplaces and the like — left behind by the expensive architect. He had to put up with it, and set about applying his delicately stencilled and painted wall schemes, designing stylish furniture, a distinctive billiard room, and all the finishing touches, including some surprising cutlery.

But this was the occasion on which Kate first used the talents of the young man who was to displace Walton as her house designer, and through his latter-day fame make her, too, famous. Charles Rennie Mackintosh (1868–1928) was at the time a young draughtsman with the architectural firm of Honeyman & Keppie. He was also, importantly, an alumnus of Glasgow School of Art, where he attended evening classes. He and his friend from work, Herbert McNair, had fallen in around 1893 with a group of young lady students at the School, and had grown particularly close to a pair of sisters, Margaret and Frances Macdonald — they later became known as 'the Four'. All these young ladies were a cut above Mackintosh socially, but offered the stimulating companionship of art and talent, heady

Young lady students of the Glasgow School of Art posing with Charles Rennie Mackintosh on an artistic outing in 1894. At the far right is Margaret Macdonald, whom Mackintosh later married, and at far left her sister Frances, who married Mackintosh's friend Herbert McNair.

notions of self-fulfilment. They called themselves the 'Immortals', and mixed youthful fooling around with seriously weird new art, all under wing of Francis, or 'Fra', Newbery, the likeable and energetic head of the School, who was dedicated to encouraging individuality, and promoting a distinctive Glasgow-grown style of design and craftwork. He had founded the Glasgow School of Art Club, whose exhibitions of paintings in recent years had established the reputations of these young artists, the Macdonalds in particular, for their notorious 'ghoulish' 'spook school' work. Newbery knew talent when he saw it, and his wife since 1889, Jessie Rowat, an embroiderer who had trained at the School and was the same age as Margaret Macdonald, was an especially devoted advocate, constantly looking for work for Mackintosh.

It may have been the Newberys who effected the introduction of Mackintosh to someone who was to prove his most loyal patron. Mackintosh's involvement was surely Miss Cranston's doing, not Walton's: although they were much the same age and had encountered each other in shared artistic circles Mackintosh does not seem to have been especially friendly with Walton, who stood somewhat apart from this School of Art group; and Walton would obviously have preferred sole control of the Buchanan Street interior, something which was of artistic importance to him. But we have seen enough of this individual woman's tastes to see what drew her to these young people who were making such a stir in art circles in Glasgow.

Perhaps this is the point at which to discuss her clothes, shown off in another portrait by James Craig Annan: she knew what she liked and obviously, more importantly, she needed to be different. She was not choosing a version of contemporary 'artistic dress' — perhaps she felt too old for that anyway — but was standing outside fashion altogether. She adopted this personal style early on as an outward sign, it seems, that she did not intend to fit in, that she rejected the controls of social norms upon the way she ran her life. Eccentricity has always had this liberating effect: if you hit people in the eye, if you just have enough panache, they won't stop you. It has normally been the upper classes, however, who have been able to escape via eccentricity in this way: to kick over the traces of conformity in the upwardly aspiring middle classes called for more nerve altogether. Glasgow was full of frustrated young middle-class women whose fathers forbade them to work, whose mothers passed on

Portrait by James Craig Annan of Kate Cranston in her prime, probably late 1890s.

constraining notions of what was proper for people in their station — they were some of the tearooms' best customers. Kate's way round this had been not to care about getting married, to be so definitely different that no one thought of applying the same standards to her. Her persistent choice of 'fancy dress' produced an entirely distinctive silhouette. As J C Annan recollected in 1938, with some confusion as to style, but evoking the general effect, she gave you the 'eerie feeling that a gracious and handsome lady had escaped from a Gainsborough, or was it a Watteau, canvas'. In fact she wore copies of 1850s Victorian dress — what her mother would have worn when Kate was a girl — very slightly adapted to reflect contemporary trends.

What was emerging in Kate in the mid 1890s was a real taste for the cutting edge of the new style. She must have liked the free spirit of the Immortals — confident young women who made their own artistic clothes, and whose 'nightmare', 'grave-yard' new art distortions produced apoplectic reactions in the local press. The extent to which Mackintosh was signalling his own inner nature and aspirations in his clothes is clear from his off-duty outfit — floppy tie, soft collar, and tweed jacket (p. 41). This was how he presented himself at Annan's studio for the well-known portraits made at this period: 'the young man as an artist'.

Kate was old enough to be Mackintosh's mother; but it was a meeting of two individuals. It was not as an architect in an office that Miss Cranston found him, but as an artist in his spare time, and this is important. She really promoted the side of him that came out so creatively in decorative work, and his work for her over the next two decades was largely in furniture and interior design. She must have seen something she liked, or perhaps she just liked the way it shocked people. It was a bold commission — to decorate the walls of the new tearooms on three floors, where they ran round a light well at the rear of the building. Mackintosh had not done anything like it before, and it was certainly going to be noticeable. On the other hand it was only paint — easy enough to obliterate if it was a complete disaster.

Mackintosh planned his scheme for unity of effect, as the different floors could be glimpsed together up the stairwell. The background colour ran from green through to greyish greenish yellow to blue, evoking an earth to sky transition, a coolish background with jewel-like spots of colour, and schematised motifs — in the lower floor, peacocks and tree shapes;

in the upper floor for the men's smoking gallery, abstract smoke ring waves, odd totemic shapes and suns (or moons); and most strikingly for the ladies' lunch gallery in the middle a frieze of statuesque white women schematically entangled with looping rose bushes and grouped with abstract tree shapes. The figures were derived from a recent watercolour by Mackintosh, entitled self-consciously *Part Seen, Imagined Part* — perhaps Miss Cranston had seen it. The scheme was perfect, transforming an area furnished with Walton's quietly artistic rush-seated ladder-back chairs into a topic of animated conversation. There was something unsettling and subconsciously sexual emanating from the weird tree forms — something that could not be talked about, but it made the gallery exciting.

The stencilling technique was probably learnt from Walton, who had developed an innovative use of stains and resists, which produced a particularly fine finish. This 'sparkling living surface' was commented upon by Gleeson White, editor of the influential art magazine, the *Studio*, who realised the novelty of these murals when he visited Glasgow to write a piece on its distinctive 'new art' in 1897. He heaped praise on the achievement of such effect through simple means, lambasting by contrast the 'extremely irritating' interior intrusions of the architect as unnecessary and costly 'eyesores'. He saw this as the first example of decor evolved through posters, a welcome change from 'the platitudes which commonly decorate restaurant walls'.

It was a terrific coup for Mackintosh, along with the Macdonalds, to get this space and this praise in the leading magazine of progressive art country-wide. (White planned to give Walton a separate write-up, but unfortunately died before he could do it.)

> To defend the work of Mr. Mackintosh is easy to one who believes in it, and it seems that belief in it should follow intimacy; for when a man has something to say and knows how to say it, the conversion of others is usually but a question of time ... so far he has justified his most ardent supporters, and there is every reason to believe that he will not disappoint them in the future.

This must have been gratifying to Kate. She had shown just this belief in both Mackintosh and Walton and had given them an opportunity to show what they could do. Already the advantage of working for Miss

Cranston was clear. It was like having your work in a popular gallery: it was open to the public all day; anyone could come and look for the price of a cup of tea. Walton had been working for some years now building up a good business, but most of his work was for private clients, hidden from general view.

Kate seems to have had excellent instincts. The outside of the building shocked no one but seemed up-to-date artistically, while inside the decor was strange and new yet stopped on this side of the outrageous, contained by Walton's sense of artistic roots and good manners, his ability overall to work within bounds. When the tearooms opened on 5 May 1897, not long before Kate's forty-eighth birthday, press approval was widespread, headed by that organ of Glasgow's influential middle-classes, the *Bailie*: 'Elegant as the new establishment is as seen from the street, its interior is no less elegant, the decorations being in excellent taste, and showing to much effect.' There was plenty to marvel at, even an elevator with a tastefully dressed attendant, and on the tables some peculiar artistic cutlery. Miss Cranston's new establishment soon became one of the 'sights of the city': visitors from out of town were taken along to be amazed by it.

One such visitor was the English architect Edwin Lutyens, who wrote to his wife-to-be Lady Emily Lytton describing how he had been taken by James Guthrie, whose firm had handled the Mackintosh work, to:

> a Miss Somebody's who is really a Mrs Somebody else. She has started a large Restaurant, all very elaborately simple on very new school High Art Lines. The result is gorgeous! and a wee bit vulgar! She has nothing but green handled knives and all is curiously painted and coloured ... Some of the knives are purple and are put as spots of colour! It is all quite good, all just a little outré, a thing we must avoid and shall too.

This slightly over-the-top quality, consistent with Glasgow's addiction at this period to conspicuous consumption and very noticeable to English eyes, is beautifully caught in Lutyens' language. But he was plainly influenced by what he saw. He was introduced to Miss Cranston and obviously raved about her special make of blue and white china, which she used throughout her establishments, a personal taste in line with current 'chinamania'. 'Most delicious blue willow pattern sets of china ware she has and as a great favour she is going to make me up a basket', he wrote to his fiancée. These became the Lutyens' breakfast things; and indeed despite his comments even green-handled knives later appeared on the family table. He also came away with the gift of 'two beautiful clay pipes, quite a joy', just right for a breakfast smoke. Here is more evidence of Kate's discrimination in providing for her customers' needs.

It was for breakfast that Lutyens made a beeline the following year, 1898, when he went straight from the train to 'these queer funny rooms'. Here he was served 'tea, butter, jam, toasts, baps and buns — 2 sausages, 2 eggs — speak it not in Gath — all for 1/1d! so clean. Most beautiful peonies on the breakfast table...' He renewed his acquaintance with Miss Cranston and this time he drew a little thumbnail sketch, and caught her neatly in words as:

> a dark, busy, fat, wee body with black sparky luminous eyes, wears a bonnet garnished with roses, and has made a fortune by supplying cheap clean foods in surroundings prompted by the New Art Glasgow School.

Lutyens sat writing in Walton's billiard room, 'all clever and original', revelling in the colours, trying to figure out the influences on this remarkably new Glasgow work, and concluding:

> So am I much amused and greatly entertained. The food! etc. at a third the cost and three times better than the ordinary hotel, and the surroundings full of space for fancy and amusement.

Lutyens put his finger right on Miss Cranston's successful formula: good value, quality and art. The tearooms were run to the highest standards of service, and provided in an economical and flexible way for both men and women, separately and together, throughout the day. Here Miss Cranston's feminine touch was coming into its own, as the *Hamilton Advertiser* commented: 'Miss Cranston knows how to cater for and please the public, and also knows better than any "mere man" what goes to the making of her own sex comfortable'. Added to these merits was decor of class and novelty, or what *Saint Mungo*, a rival to the *Bailie* in these years, referred to more or less affectionately as 'weirdry'. Glasgow was ready for this, proud of having produced something else special.

Indeed Glasgow's urban life was achieving a new sophistication all round. The Corporation was getting its teeth into municipal improvements and visitors came from far and wide to observe this model of civic intervention: in 1894, for instance, one of the country's first sewage farms was opened — not before time, given the disgusting pollution of the Clyde. Plans were afoot too for some cultural provisions on a scale felt to be long overdue for a city of this importance. In 1897 the foundation stone was laid for a grand new Art Gallery and Museum in Kelvingrove Park, funded partly with the proceeds of the 1888 exhibition. The city's poorer classes were not forgotten, and the People's Palace, opened in 1898 and immediately avidly used, was going up on Glasgow Green to house art and other amenities for the inhabitants of Glasgow's East End. Meanwhile Mackintosh's design had won the competition early in 1897 for a new art school for the city (originally proposed as part of the Art Gallery and Museum, but now going ahead as a separate project). A proposal to mount a second International Exhibition to inaugurate the new Art Gallery in the first year of the next century found enthusiastic backers. Miss Cranston took note and mentally resolved to be there.

This was the height of the tearoom boom: new tearooms were opening on all sides and in 1897 journalists just couldn't keep off the subject. 'Anyone would judge from the number of tea-rooms sprouting everywhere that these, aesthetic or otherwise, must be profitable concerns', wrote *St Mungo* in October 1897. Like other crazes of the day — vegetarianism and female bicycling — the new tearooms seemed subtly subversive of the old order. In 'The spread of the insidious tea-room' (17 November 1897), the *Bailie* lamented the demise of the good old 'pint of bitter and a dressed steak', and accused the tearooms of turning out a new kind of roué, the clerk of artistic temperament, ruined by a mixture of tea, tobacco, talk and pretty waitresses. The attractions of tearoom waitresses in particular made excellent copy. In this recognisable social change Miss Cranston led the way, and the 'artistic' nature of the tearooms was widely imitated.

The opening of Buchanan Street, which became the showpiece and headquarters of Miss Cranston's business, brought a significant increase in the number of her employees and a need to restructure management. Buchanan Street with its billiard room offered extended leisure facilities reflecting the general trends of social life. In 1899 Mackintosh designed a card for Miss Cranston advertising music from Mr Rubini Rochester's sextet on Tuesdays and Thursdays during the winter months — a 'palm court' background to clinking cups was something that the department stores took up keenly in their competitive efforts to woo customers. (Mr Rochester was a Barrhead acquaintance — he was the organist of the Evangelical Union Church that the Cochranes attended, and a pillar of the Barrhead Choral Union.) Trusted manageresses ran the separate branches, while Kate established the routine which was to make her such a familiar figure to thousands of her fellow-citizens, walking briskly between her three premises each day to cast her eagle eye over all aspects of their functioning.

However as soon as Buchanan Street was open and running she turned her attention to her next plan. This was to expand substantially at 114 Argyle Street where she had her original establishment. The lease for the whole building, ie for the temperance hotel above as well as the ground floor premises occupied by the tearooms, is said to have been her husband's wedding present to her, but this is not really supported by the Valuation Rolls which record the owners and tenants of properties. It seems more likely, if the story has a germ of truth in it, that the Buchanan Street building, which was bought in 1894, was such a present — John Cochrane evidently understood and appreciated his wife's ambitions, though if it was sentiment that prompted the gesture it proved to be a shrewd investment notwithstanding.

The building at Argyle Street belonged to the Scottish Provident Institution at this point, but Miss Cranston took over the full lease around 1895. The hotel ran on as the Crown Temperance hotel under a tenant for a year or so from 1896–7. Did Kate at some point have the intention of running it as a hotel? Possibly, but the successful launch of Buchanan Street certainly justified her decision that in these boom years the space would be more profitably used as another large suite of tearooms. Again attention was paid to providing enhanced amenities for men, with billiard tables to add to the smoking and coffee facilities which were so much used during business hours. This was essentially a working part of town. Argyle Street had plenty of shops — including the famed Royal Polytechnic opened by John Anderson, pioneer of the 'universal store' with his policy of buying in bulk and selling cheap — though this did not now have the cachet of the newer stores on Sauchiehall Street.

Plans for recasting 114 Argyle Street were drawn up in 1897 and work started on the project in the middle of 1898: a smoking room with a separate entrance was opened that year, while work on the rest of the building went on into 1899. It was a thorough overhaul, and could not be completed without another injection of cash.

Kate's father George died at home in Barrhead in January 1899, leaving an estate of only £225, which was sorted out by Stuart as his next of kin (George's older sons had evidently disappeared from his life by this stage). At the same time his daughter was going back to John Stewart for another £2000 against Buchanan Street. She raised the money to complete the work on Argyle Street — but it meant that she had a very large mortgage, £16000 in all, to service. She did own the building by 1913, when in the Valuation Rolls 'Mrs Catherine Cochrane' is listed as the proprietor, and 'Catherine Cranston, tea room keeper' as the occupant — an interesting proof of the separation she kept between her private and her business life.

Kate asked George Walton again to handle the interior decoration and this time she seems to have learnt from the mistakes at Buchanan Street where the Edinburgh architect's intrusive embellishments in the interior were a costly hindrance to the kind of job that Walton would have liked to do. For Argyle Street she chose Glasgow architects who had made a name building schools to revamp the outside of the building — though the pretty entrance with its beaten metalwork rose motif was evidently Walton's work. The architects deleted the hotel's old tenement appearance with a grey harled exterior and some fanciful gables and dormers — the look was described as 'Belgian'. But they left the interior a bare, featureless shell, which gave Walton full play for some stylish fittings: he provided some of his particularly attractive new art fireplaces, and panelling incorporating leaded glass (stained glass was another decorative field in which his company was doing particularly innovative work), as well as characteristic stencilled decoration on the walls. It was a fine showcase for the company's capabilities.

This time Miss Cranston seems deliberately to have let Mackintosh loose on the furniture. Again she must have seen some of the few pieces he had designed by this time (a linen press and a chest of drawers were illustrated in the *Studio* article which had broadcast Mackintosh's Buchanan Street work) or talked to him about what interested him. But

George Walton's street entrance to Miss Cranston's premises at 114 Argyle Street,
reopened in much expanded form in 1899.

the commission to furnish the new tearooms was much the biggest
furniture design job he had handled.

Some of what he produced was in the simple, broadly Arts and Crafts
style of his earlier furniture, sturdy, though finished with distinctive
refinement. But working with Walton provoked him again to competitive
individualism, and there were stunningly innovative elements in what he
designed, most notably the tall-backed chair with oval headpiece which
has become a design classic. It had that quality of overstatement that
seemed to work for Miss Cranston. Mackintosh later used this chair in his
own dining room, so he was evidently pleased with it himself — he had
other pieces of tearoom furniture in his house too. Like many others
Mackintosh was to design for Miss Cranston, this chair had its structural
defects, but it was unquestionably striking, and together with Walton's
contributions, including the luxurious decorative mosaic 'Eros' panel,
gave the lunch room its special ambience.

Mackintosh, who must have learnt from Walton, went on to other
jobs in interior design including furniture after this commission: Kate

can be seen to have given him the opportunity to expand his creative range in a way that was to prove immensely fruitful for him. The new Argyle Street tearooms opened late in 1899, another important step in the process of gaining new consumers for the 'Glasgow Style' among the city's affluent middle classes. The large furniture firm of Wylie & Lochhead took notice and began to promote furniture in this up-to-date and distinctive style alongside the range of revivalist designs it had on offer.

As the century turned Glasgow looked forward with confidence to continuing progress and prosperity. Miss Cranston's business was flourishing, and in 1900 she moved on unhesitatingly to her premises at Ingram Street, wishing to bring them into line with her others with stylistic updating and enlarged facilities. She took over the ground floor premises at numbers 213–15, previously occupied by Jeyes Sanitary Compound Company — a clear example of the way service industries were moving into commercial areas. Providing again for both sexes she planned a ladies' luncheon room on the ground floor, while the basement space below was to be given over to a new billiard and smoking room for men — billiards was something of a male craze at this period.

On this occasion however Kate gave the whole interior design job to Mackintosh, by-passing George Walton. This may have been chiefly because Walton had by now moved to London, joining the talent drain from which Glasgow and Scotland at large has traditionally suffered; he was following his older brother E A Walton and others of the Glasgow Boys group, who were now established as fashionable painters. He had sold his private company and launched George Walton & Co, Ltd in 1897 — Miss Cranston showed her confidence by buying £100 of shares — and although he still worked with the company in Glasgow, he had been handling the Argyle Street work partly at a distance, which cannot have been altogether satisfactory for a demanding employer. But Kate was also coming to know Mackintosh and was obviously pleased with him: perhaps she had seen the white bedroom he designed probably late in 1898 at Westdel, Dowanhill, for the Glasgow publisher Robert Maclehose; and then there was the School of Art, opened at the end of 1899, a thoroughly impressive achievement. There was a growing personal regard between these two strong characters, who shared perfectionism, and a sense of humour. And Kate obviously had a taste for that something extra that Mackintosh gave her in design terms.

So Mackintosh did not have to work with Walton. Instead he worked closely with someone whose artistic ideas melded with his, his with hers. Mackintosh and Margaret Macdonald had been deeply attached for some years, and she and her sister had been a strong influence on his artistic development. Frances had married Herbert McNair the previous year. In August Mackintosh was to marry Margaret. The job for Miss Cranston was done in same spurt of creativity and involvement with interior design (and with each other) in which they furnished and decorated their future home at Mains Street.

This was not just a shop-fitting design job — it was hands on and very creative. In April Mackintosh wrote to his supporter Hermann Muthesius that he was very busy: 'I have been out each morning this week at 6 o'clock decorating the barricade'. He was borrowing Walton's idea of making something artistic of the hoarding. In July he wrote that he was 'not nearly done with "Miss Cranstons" yet it has involved a great lot of work'. He and Margaret were in the middle of working on two large decorative gesso panels, which were to face each other across the lunch room: 'We are working them together and that makes the work very pleasant.'

Kate's commission of 'his and hers' decorative panels from them — two in gesso, two in silvered lead — was effectively a wedding present to the young couple, the best they could have, a practical and yet artistic boost to the beginning of their joint life. She let them take the panels to Vienna in October to form part of their exhibit at the Vienna Secession, which made a strong impression on the avant garde there.

This was genuine artistic patronage, because the work was so personal and creative. There were plenty of discriminating art collectors in Glasgow at this period — William Burrell is perhaps the best known — industrialists and magnates with varied tastes including a general penchant for paintings of the Barbizon school, and the city's own Glasgow Boys; they bought from dealers like Alexander Reid, a friend of Van Gogh. We do not know whether Miss Cranston went in for buying any such 'art': what is clear is the pleasure she took in supporting applied artists and sharing their work by channelling it into her tearooms, open to all. She, like her designers, approached the room as a work of art.

At same time this patronage created something with value — a special atmosphere. Stepping from the grubby soot-stained street outside into

The Ladies Luncheon Room at the Ingram Street tearooms, created by Mackintosh and Margaret Macdonald in 1900. Here as reconstructed by Glasgow Museums for the 1996–7 Mackintosh exhibition; installation by Los Angeles County Museum of Art.

the creamy white luncheon room at Ingram Street, with its silvery gleams and pretty dabs of colour, impeccably white tablecloths, fresh flowers and carefully laid tables, was a special experience which worked its magic even on people who would never have lived with such stuff. So it gave Miss Cranston's tearooms individuality and meaning, and every new decorative scheme topped up her high profile. The room as a work of art was a valuable business asset.

5

'A gey smert wumman': Miss Cranston to the fore

As 1900 drew to a close there was growing excitement in Glasgow, for the city was preparing in earnest for its next great International Exhibition in 1901. The argument that this would be the first major exhibition of the twentieth century, since logically 1900 was the last year of the nineteenth, was well supported in Glasgow, predictably enough. It was Paris that had bagged 1900. Glasgow was ready now to compete at this world city level and Kelvingrove Park was taken over again for what was billed as the largest exhibition in Britain to date.

One aim was to inaugurate the new Art Gallery and Museum, which had been built partly with the profits of the last exhibition. More generally the exhibition was to express satisfaction with the achievements of the past and a confident interest in the future: it would show progress in Art, Industry and Science during the nineteenth century and provide 'a resting place for pioneers' from which they could start forth again with new courage and inspiration. The death of Queen Victoria in January of 1901 as preparations were getting serious seemed to confirm the ending of an era and the beginning of something new. The visible exempla of progress this time were automobiles and telephones — just as electricity had stolen the show in 1888. As before the exhibition was made a deadline for getting things done. The newly electrified Corporation tramcars made a strong impression on outsiders, and a municipal telephone system was up and running as a competitor to the National Telephone Company. Glasgow's vigorous municipalisation of services was indeed one thing the city desired to show off, and there was much to be marvelled at outside as well as inside the exhibition.

Glasgow's industries, centring round its magnificent ships and locomotives, were of course powerfully impressive, while in cultural matters the city had developed rapid assurance since the last exhibition. Its homegrown 'school' of painting, not really a school but a group of recognisably like-minded artists, had achieved wide recognition. The Glasgow School of Art, recently moved into its brand new Mackintosh-designed building on Renfrew Street, was nationally prominent and was promoting very effectively the importance of design education for industry and the achievements of designers in the applied arts. A 'Glasgow Style' was becoming widely recognisable — something to which Miss Cranston had made a significant contribution.

Strangers to the city were struck by its distinctive tearooms, and if they bought the little *Glasgow in 1901* by 'J H Muir' — a pseudonym for three bright young men, Archibald Hamilton Charteris, James Bone and his brother, the artist Muirhead Bone — they found in it a penetrating description of the phenomenon. The proliferation of these places in the last decade was such that Glasgow could now be dubbed 'a very Tokio for tea rooms'. The book describes the pleasure and relief of a Clyde Scot returning from London, bereft of such establishments, 'to where he may lunch on lighter fare than steak and porter for the sum of fivepence amid surroundings which remind him of a pleasant home'. It comments on the broad spectrum of middle-class society, male and female, which used the tearooms throughout the day, and the comfortable democracy of the smoking room where clerks and bosses mingled easily. The tearooms were generally remarkable for their location (often in previously unused basements) and 'the scheme of their decorations'. For as we have seen, Kate Cranston's example had encouraged many women to begin their own modest businesses in imitation, while her particular brand of artistic taste had established a distinctive tearoom style. (Although none of her imitators went so far as to employ Mackintosh, a generally feminine artistic style prevailed, using for instance fashionable Liberty fabrics, Japanese matting, and stencilled decoration.) Domestic niceties like wooden tables 'spread with fair white cloths and set with flowers and china' were the norm, and contrasted by 'Muir' with the bleak marble of an Edinburgh café or a London ABC teashop. For men there were the added attractions of the waitresses.

It was natural that Miss Cranston should represent this important Glasgow phenomenon at the exhibition itself — putting the artistic tearoom on show as it were — and she had seen a good commercial opportunity. This kind of speculative expenditure apparently did not appeal to her brother Stuart: at all events he did not take space himself, though a rival tea dealer, Flint's, who had opened an 'artistic' tearoom in town, had an elegant little place on site, along with the bigger catering contractors. The main exhibition buildings had been executed in a frothy, vaguely oriental style, and it was left to some of the minor buildings to strike a more up-to-date architectural note.

Kate had secured a prime site right in front of the new Art Gallery, served by a special footbridge across the Kelvin, for what became her famed 'tea house and tea terrace'. It was a long white structure flanked by two towers, the rooms on the ground floor 'tastefully decorated', the terrace above shaded with hops, creepers and flowers. It backed in an ungainly way onto the great shell-shaped bandstand which faced the Art Gallery. There is no record of who designed or decorated it for her. It could have been Mackintosh; or maybe it was Walton, who certainly designed the menu card, his last known work for Kate. Both designers were skilled at creating stylish effects from cheap materials, which is what was needed.

Whoever it was, Miss Cranston's exhibition tearoom, an important showcase, obviously reflected the style of her city-centre branches. As Neil Munro — novelist, 'Prince of Glasgow journalists' and, as we have seen, another of Miss Cranston's admirers — recalled, its 'architectural and decorative innovations created a sensation even among continental visitors'. A measure of Kate's recent rise to prominence and visibility was the new expression overheard on the exhibition site, reported by 'J H Muir': 'Oh, it'll do A1! it's quite Kate Cranstonish!'. 'Kate Cranstonish', according to Neil Munro, 'became a term with Glasgow people in general to indicate domestic novelties in buildings and decorations not otherwise easy to define'.

This was remembered as another long summer of enjoyment and pleasure. The fair weather was a blessing from the gods — Kate's terrace would not have been so popular in one of the rainy cold summers that

FROM THE WEST.

A view of Glasgow's 1901 International Exhibition in Kelvingrove Park, showing Miss Cranston's elegant white Tea House and Terrace served by a special bridge over the Kelvin. To the right is the newly built Kelvingrove Art Gallery and Museum, and in the background the temporary structure of the exhibiton's main building. In the foreground is the much-loved switchback ride.

they often dished out for Glasgow; but the gods took with the other hand when the tearoom was struck by fire, a perpetual risk in these temporary buildings, and burnt down on 8 July. Miss Cranston seems to have risen to the occasion; in fact she was doubtless in her element dealing with the unexpected problems of running these exceptional premises. A temporary marquee was erected and the building was resurrected at speed, though it was not finished quite so elegantly as before. However there was an urgent need for its restitution, as the provision for refreshments within the exhibition was proving generally unequal to the number of visitors — there was about twice the attendance of 1888, a staggering eleven million, while the capacity of the restaurants was not very much greater. After the success of the first exhibition many more locals had bought season tickets to make use of the exhibition as a summer amenity. Glaswegians now were used to the pleasures of a nice tea; they were more used to pleasure in general. Kate might have fretted at not being able to make better use of an opportunity.

As the year drew towards its close the exhibition was cleared away, and life got back to normal, not without a sense of loss. Kate Cranston turned her sights back to the city centre. Glasgow was still going west, and Sauchiehall Street was clearly the new place to be. It was described by *Glasgow in 1901* as 'the brightest and gayest street in Glasgow, the only street of pleasure. It has more painted buildings and gilded signs than any other, and its sky-line is more irregular, piquant, and full of contrasts.' Sauchiehall Street had taken off in the 1890s as the new department stores established themselves there, shifting the centre of gravity of shopping in Glasgow. Copland and Lye had been there from as early as 1878; Pettigrew and Stephens, founded in 1888, was completing major expansions in 1901 (Mackintosh had a hand in the designs); Daly's had been established in 1897; Walter Wilson, whose Colosseum in Jamaica Street was in a less elegant part of town, was now moving straight upmarket, building his enormous, sophisticated 'Tréron & Cie' round the old Corporation Art Galleries, which had been abandoned for the new building in Kelvingrove (today restored to civic use as the McLellan Galleries).

Operating on the 'American system' of allowing customers to walk through and look without being importuned to buy, the new stores had burgeoned. With their own tearooms, palm court orchestras, rest rooms and lavish decor they were wooing females with money and time to spend. Shopping was now a central leisure activity, often built round meeting friends for lunch or tea in a delightful tearoom. There were other well-known ladies' haunts on Sauchiehall Street, like Assafrey's, the long-established chocolatier, and Skinner's at the Charing Cross end; but there was plenty of room for competition. Property values were rising but not yet as high as in Buchanan Street. Miss Cranston acquired the lease for number 217, a tenement next to Daly's, valued in the rolls at £2900.

The location called for something a bit smart and special, both inside and out, and this is what she asked for and got from the Mackintoshes. Public expectations were piqued again with a strange and elegant hoarding, which advertised the opening of the new tea and lunch rooms in October 1903. Behind it builders got on with transforming the old stone facade to Mackintosh's designs, so that it emerged looking like a completely new building, smartly stuccoed and painted, with a shallow curving bay on its front, glittering odd-shaped windows, and strings of chic squares to pick out its lines.

This was another chance for Mackintosh to exercise his craving for complete control of a project. 'Miss Cranston is delighted with everything I have suggested', he wrote to Anna Muthesius on 27 March 1903 when work was starting; 'she thinks this is going to be by far her first place'. And this, tellingly, was in the same letter in which, collapsing into the role of victim which sometimes tempted him, he complained of times when 'antagonisms and undeserved ridicule, bring on feelings of despondency and despair'. It was all right to attract the boorish contempt of the stuffy press when you were a young student with your talents just bursting out; but by this stage it was becoming a bit wearing trying to make a living and maintain artistic integrity at the same time. What bliss it must have been to work for Miss Cranston. It would be fascinating to know more of their working relationship. There is no evidence of her making any difficulties or imposing constraints. This is really surprising when there are plenty of other indications that she was a stickler for things being done her way, and being done properly. We can only assume that she was astute enough to recognise the real thing and to know that Mackintosh needed his head if he was to work at his best. It is as if Kate's own single-minded perfectionism tuned in to that same quality in Mackintosh, which to lesser clients made him arrogant about his work and almost unemployable.

What Mackintosh would have done without Kate Cranston becomes an increasingly relevant question after this. What he could do for her was well exemplified for now in the perfect art-house tearoom that he created for her. The Willow Tea Rooms were finished in time for opening as advertised on 29 October in 1903 — a considerable achievement.

The press response was all Kate might have hoped for. The *Evening News* thought Miss Cranston's new establishment 'the acme of originality', while the *Bailie*, arbiter of middle-class taste, wrote:

Hitherto Miss Cranston has been famous for the daintily artistical character of her several establishments. However her new establishment fairly outshines all others in the matters of arrangement and colour. The furnishing, besides, is of the richest and most luxurious character. Indeed Miss Cranston has carried the question of comfort fairly into that of luxury, when providing for the enjoyment of her friends and patrons. Her "Salon de luxe" on the first floor is simply a marvel of the art of the upholsterer and decorator. And not less admirable, each in its own way, are the tea-gallery, the lunch-rooms, the billiard-room, and the smoking room.

Here was praise and fame indeed — for Miss Cranston. The approval of the Mackintoshes' work is obvious, but so too is their anonymity: it is Miss Cranston who walks off with the credit. And after all she paid for it: this is how it works. But one can understand how embittering this lack of recognition must have become to Mackintosh over the years. This is how the image of the artist as misunderstood hero arises: proper recognition comes only years later, when the patron is forgotten. But as far as the work itself is concerned it is a partnership between the enabler and the doer. Thanks to both Miss Cranston and Mackintosh this gem was made, photographed, and used, and although it was later lost, it has now been partially recreated for an admiring public to enjoy.

The Willow was not very big but it was exquisite. Inside, the somewhat extravagant style explored round these years by Mackintosh and Margaret struck a note quite suitable for the purpose. Much of the building was open plan; the light separation of its different areas by devices of various kinds allowed the essential eating out experience of seeing and being seen. The spaces were differentiated and yet coordinated by their decorative schemes: white, pink and silver for the ladies' tearoom; dark grey canvas panelling with touches of pink in the stencilled decorations for the rear lunch room; lighter grey, white and pink for the general tea gallery.

The intensity was concentrated to wonderful excess in the Salon de luxe, soon popularly known as the Room de luxe, a kind of glittering treasure-box of specialness, the ultimate example of the tearoom as a work of art. Even the waitresses seem to have been particularly pretty, dressed by Mackintosh in white with shawl collars, and chokers of big pink beads, evoking a slightly eighteenth-century look. Margaret had contributed a decorative panel, in her favourite medium of gesso: three droopy ladies, liberally looped with strings of glass jewels, the title making at least a literary connection with the willow theme which ran lightly

Two of Miss Cranston's carefully chosen waitresses, in costumes designed by Mackintosh, sitting at a table in the 'Room de Luxe' in the Willow Tea Rooms.

through the interior schemes — 'O ye, all ye that walk in Willow-wood'. The chairs were silver, with purple seats. Above was a chandelier of innumerable pink glass baubles, bewitching to generations of small children, remembered by the young Mary Newbery as 'absolutely perfectly beautiful'. Round the walls ran a frieze of leaded purple, white and mirror glass, reflecting back the customers of this beautiful princessy world.

We have an interesting insight into how much Miss Cranston spent on all this. Although the figures in modern terms seem laughably small, they represent significant outlay in relation to what might normally be spent on equipping a new restaurant. Each of these leaded glass panels in the Room de luxe had cost Miss Cranston £1. The eight high-backed chairs in the centre of the room were £2 16s 0d apiece — expensive compared with the ladderbacks downstairs, of which there were 137 at 17s 6d each. But she quickly recouped her extra investment, not only through an extra penny on a cup of tea (3d rather than 2d elsewhere in the establishment), but through the business benefits of notoriety.

This was all well over the top, but it was in keeping with a new Edwardian spirit of enjoyment, looking to the future, casting off a heavy Victorian past. These were years of theatres, music halls, new cinemas, dancing — and of course eating out. To Glasgow it must have seemed that the city was launched into its most prosperous decade ever — and so it was in some ways, but it was just not solid enough: the economic base was already being fatally damaged by foreign competition.

On the surface, though, people were out for new experiences, and the Willow was certainly that. Even if people actually thought of it as 'too much', they enjoyed the whole extravagant ambience. Neil Munro captured this amused admiration in his regular column in the *Evening News*. In 'Erchie in an art tea-room', he exposes two working-class Glaswegians to 'the refining and elevating influence of Miss Cranston's beautiful rooms'. The interplay between his two characters is deftly humorous: Erchie, a waiter, has pretensions to knowledge of the world, while Duffy, a coalman, is completely out of his depth. He was on the way to a pub to spend the insurance money he'd got for a dead horse, when Erchie caught him, and for a joke steered him to 'thon new tea-room wi' the comic windows'. Duffy gapes at it:

> "Michty!" says he, "wha did this?" "Miss Cranston," says I, "Was she tryin'?" says Duffy. "She took baith hands to't," I tellt him. "And a gey smert wumman too if ye ask me."

Erchie gets Duffy through the door, cap in hand. 'He gave the wan look roond him, and put his hand in his pooch to feel his money'; but

Erchie assures him it will cost no more than the pub, and they climb the stairs. Even the suave Erchie is a little quelled by the interior:

> I may tell ye I was a wee bit put aboot mysel'… There was naething in the hale place was the way I was accustomed to; the very snecks o' the doors were kind o' contrairy. "This way for the threepenny cups and the guid bargains," says I to Duffy, and I lands him into what they ca' the Room de Looks…

There follows an amusing description of Mackintosh's decoration through Erchie's eyes, eg:

> The chairs is no' like ony other chairs ever I clapped eyes on, but ye could easy guess they were chairs; and a' roond the place there's a lump o' lookin'-gless wi' purple leeks pented on it every noo and then.

However the waitress is recognisably a pretty girl, causing Duffy to quip that this must be the 'Room de Good Looks', and he perks up. He is disconcerted to think he has a defective teaspoon — 'till I tellt him that was whit made it Art. "Art," says he, "whit the mischief's Art". Erchie then describes ruefully how 'Art' broke out in his own home when his wife was taken by artistic tastes, threw out all the old things and replaced them with what was now acceptable. Now it's 'ragin' a' ower the place'.

Driven by the desire for that staple of the Glasgow high tea, a mutton pie, the pair descend again to the 'solid food department': the dining room at the rear of the ground floor. Here the system of ordering food from the basement kitchen with colour-coded balls popped down a pipe is another source of wonderment to Duffy — but as Erchie continues:

> 'That's Art. Ye can hae yer pie frae the kitchen withoot them yellin' doon a pipe for't and lettin' a' the ither customers ken whit ye want.' When the pie cam' up, it was jist the shape o' an ordinary pie, wi' nae beads nor onything Art aboot it, and Duffy cheered up at that, and said he enjoyed his tea.

The Willow might have been a subject of mirth, but it really caught the public imagination too, the spirit of the times. And what is more, it served a good high tea.

6

'A real patron and friend'

During this time the Cochranes had been living in Barrhead in a comfortable but comparatively modest semi-detached house on the Carlibar Road. Money and energy had been poured into the tearooms: there were now four substantial establishments, and Kate had been fully occupied with creating them, one after the other, over the last decade. Things were going well, the tearooms were repaying handsomely the effort and money invested in them: despite paying for the Willow in 1903 Kate was able to pay off £2000 of her mortgage on Buchanan Street.

In Barrhead the engineering business founded by her husband's father in 1850 and now run by John and two younger brothers was still doing well. The Grahamston works, manufacturing boilers and a profitable line in gold-crushing machinery for South African gold mines, was the second largest enterprise in the town, conferring status and civic responsibilities upon its owners. When Barrhead became a burgh in 1894 John Cochrane had naturally been elected to the Town Council. It was a matter of dispute as to which of the town's three leading industrial eminences would become first Provost: in the event John Cochrane was beaten by Willie Shanks, the head of the great sanitary-ware firm which brought wide fame to Barrhead. After Shanks came Zecariah John Heys, who died in office in 1902. There was no question then that the third provost should be John Cochrane: he was duly elected and was to serve until 1907. So altogether it seemed time now for the Cochranes to spend something on their domestic surroundings: the success they had separately achieved, and their social standing, asked for somewhere a little grander.

In 1904 they moved to a fine thick-walled old mansion house — Hous'hill, set on an estate at Nitshill, between Barrhead and Glasgow, convenient for both businesses. It dated back to the seventeenth century or beyond: James Graham of Claverhouse allegedly lived or at least stayed there. It was a long low house with a terrace running its full length, adorned by strutting peacocks. (It is quite likely that the peacocks came with the house, but Kate might have imported them, as a suitably flamboyant jeu d'esprit: the peacock was a popular aesthetic motif.)

This was another leased property — renting rather than buying was common at this period — but Kate set about redoing it to suit her taste. Which meant Mackintosh, just as ten years before when she moved into East Park it had meant Walton.

Miss Cranston's instinct for staying out in front of the competition could explain the advanced design she commissioned for her business premises: it was part of what was special about having tea in her tearooms, the chance to play at inhabiting avant-garde surroundings you would not want to live in every day. But this private commission to Mackintosh shows that Kate Cranston really meant it: she — and presumably her husband — *did* want to live with some of the most advanced design in Europe at this period.

The Cochranes had very probably been invited to Walter Blackie's new Hill House in Helensburgh, which was finished early in 1904, to see what Mackintosh could do given his head on a domestic job — just as the Blackies must have taken a close look at the Ingram Street tearooms when they were thinking about employing Mackintosh in 1902. The Cochranes would have found another enthusiastic patron and a family well pleased by their fine new 'dwelling house' on its hill.

The Cochranes' Hous'hill was there already of course — Mackintosh did not have the kind of free hand he would most have liked. But as an interior design job it was a big one, covering the furnishing and decoration of the hall, dining room, drawing room, and two bedrooms. As with the Blackies there were some items of existing furniture that had to be accommodated in the schemes, including the piano designed by George Walton a decade earlier, which Mackintosh put behind a curved screen of fins making a music area at one end of the drawing room. His designing

The Cochranes' bedroom, designed by Mackintosh, at Hous'hill.

was becoming increasingly absorbed with the decorative use of the square, influenced by Vienna. It is odd to remember that Miss Cranston moved among all this dressed still in the fussy ruffles of fifty years before, in piquant contrast to furniture and fittings in a quite extraordinarily streamlined or geometric style.

Mackintosh used to say that no architect could make a home for someone he did not know well, though he could make a house. He knew Miss Cranston well by now and there was a trust and a mutual regard between them. That they got on easily was recalled for Alistair Moffat by Peter Davidson over a trip to Hous'hill to install some card-table candlesticks which he had made to Mackintosh's exacting design. Miss Cranston, characteristically perhaps, arrived first at the station, and Mackintosh came last with a flourish of his cape. There was good-humoured banter. 'The entire turn-out was so like Mackintosh and Miss Cranston seemed to be delighted with it all'.

What comes across is a sense of her liveliness and Mackintosh's pleasure in putting on a show for her. According to Davidson Kate frequently wore 'a mist-grey corduroy costume, smartly cut and a small bowler hat to match', and you could not help looking at her as she walked along Sauchiehall Street.

In 1903 Mackintosh had landed an sizeable job when he was appointed to design the Scotland Street School in Glasgow — perhaps through the good offices of Kate's cousin Mary Mason, who was on the School Board. This ran on over the next few years. But otherwise work was beginning to dry up for Mackintosh: it was the end of the tide of major commissions. A lot of jobs over the last years had come from Miss Cranston as she expanded her empire, and now that empire was largely complete. Tearooms in general ceased to multiply so prolifically: while new businesses still appeared, others closed. In Glasgow at large the period of exciting growth had finished and the building boom ran out. The city was still growing, but more slowly now, and it no longer ranked as Europe's sixth city. In fact, although the general prosperity and gaiety of the Edwardian years obscured it, the steam had gone out of Glasgow's economy: there was an underlying decline as competition made inroads into Glasgow's traditional industries and markets.

As for Miss Cranston, four branches were enough for her: she had no more major expansions in sight. However it was important for her to keep her image up to date, to maintain her leading reputation, and over the remaining Edwardian years she found a succession of small extensions and refurbishing jobs for Mackintosh to do. In part it was because she loved to be doing something new, but she was prompted too, it seems, by a personal loyalty to Mackintosh, for really almost single-handedly she kept him afloat over the next decade, able to work and more importantly to develop his style in new directions — the gift of creative life. In this she showed herself, as Mary Newbery Sturrock said, 'a real patron and friend'.

At the Argyle Street tearooms, still popular with men (it was here for instance that *Saint Mungo's* columnist wrote in 1905 'I have attained that state of aesthetic satisfaction which is associated in my mind only with M— C—'s lunch room'), Miss Cranston decided to convert a basement into an additional tearoom. It was to be called the Dutch Kitchen. Mackintosh started on it at the end of 1905 and work went on through the next year.

It was probably Kate who thought of the theme — maybe she had collected some Delft tiles she wanted to use. But the result is probably a good indication of how little she interfered, because apart from a stylish ingleneuk arrangement with tiled fireplace, and a heavily raftered black ceiling there was nothing cosy or kitcheny about it. The effect can be well described as urban chic. There was a swirl of pink in the rose motif in the leaded windows, and the Windsor chairs were a surprising strong green, but otherwise everything was black and white and decorated with Viennesey squares, making the eyes dance under the electric lights. Niches were scooped out of the plaster to take vases, one of Mackintosh's favourite devices to allow scope for Miss Cranston's love of flowers.

The next year, 1907, was quite busy: Mackintosh started work on the completion and extension of the Glasgow School of Art, while Miss Cranston threw in a request for an extension at Ingram Street. She had acquired the lease for number 217 on the corner with Miller Street. Here he made the masculine Oak Room out of an awkward tall thin space, with a billiard room in the basement. The design, with its dark wooden structures decorated with chamfering and wavy lathes and spots of colour, had much in common with the ideas developed in the renowned School of Art library at this time, and shows Mackintosh absorbed with new ideas.

However he had to spin out supervision of the School of Art job over 1908 because he had practically nothing else on his books, and 1909 seemed just as empty, apart from finishing off the School, which was finally opened in December 1909. So Kate Cranston looked around at Ingram Street and found two peculiar little disregarded spaces for him to exercise his ingenuity upon. He made from them an Oval Room, as a kind of extension opening off the Oak Room, and below it a ladies' rest room aimed at the increasing number of 'business ladies' brought into existence by the spread of the typewriter. Casting around at home, Kate came up with a commission for a card room at Hous'hill, together with some other odd jobs, which Mackintosh eked out into 1910.

Kate had made one other significant business expansion, but it was at a practical level and did not require any decorative finish: in 1908 she acquired property on the corner of St Vincent Street and Pitt Street, which in the following year was converted to make a bakery, laundry and stables. This was a significant change to the way she ran things, and presumably led to economies of scale and less buying-in of services. The stabling was for the horses which delivered supplies to the branches: Miss Cranston's modernity did not extent to the current fascination with motor vehicles.

Despite this outgoing she paid off another £2000 of the mortgage on Buchanan Street in 1910.

An up-to-date bakery and laundry, and in-house delivery facilities formed a valuable back-up resource when, with another new king awaiting coronation, Glasgow's next big exhibition came into view. A Scottish Exhibition of National History, Art and Industry was to be staged in Kelvingrove Park in 1911: there was now an unquenchable appetite for these mega shows. Looking back it might seem that the displacing of industry by history, and of outward-looking internationalism by a more introverted patriotism was symptomatic of a dangerous complacency. The fun of the exhibition disguised a slump in Glasgow's locomotive and shipbuilding industries as they failed to adapt to foreign competition: strikes in 1911 and 1912 were ominous indicators of disruption to come.

Meantime the organisers of the exhibition learnt from complaints made in 1901 and responded to changes which had taken place in society over the intervening Edwardian years by laying on plenty of entertainments, including an aerial railway, a mountain scenic railway and a 'mysterious river' ride, together with other amusements in thin educational disguise, such as villages of West Africans and of Laplanders, and a fake Highland village populated by Scotland's own quaint Gaelic-speaking natives. There was also a wonderful bogus Auld Toon, all made out of fibrous plaster like the rest of the exhibition's magnificent buildings, complete with retailing outlets — a forerunner of the attractively tidy, consumer-oriented 'living history' displays of today's theme parks.

This time Miss Cranston made no mistake and bid for the franchise for two patriotically named tearooms — the White Cockade above the Grand Amphitheatre, and the Red Lion overlooking the music court in the baronial look plasterboard Palace of Industry. At both these tearooms customers could sit out on the balconies and enjoy their refreshments to the strains of the band music that was so popular in public places at this period. Once again it was an abnormally brilliant summer. Glaswegians were now more vocal about what they wanted, and there were complaints about the level of catering — stale cakes and 'food fit only for a hungry schoolboy': Miss Cranston, however, was normally excepted from such accusations.

This exhibition gave Kate another chance to help out Mackintosh, who had had practically nothing to do the previous year, and who had begun to suffer spells of depression, expressed in and exacerbated by heavy drinking. This was evidently not something that Miss Cranston took a high moral line on: she was an abstainer herself but not a virulently crusading one — whisky, brandy and sherry were kept, under lock and key, in the tearooms for culinary purposes. She did not preach temperance at people, though her tearooms, as was often acknowledged, had furthered the cause more practically than any number of tracts.

Mackintosh designed the interior of the White Cockade tearoom, while Margaret produced a very smart menu card. Placing commissions diplomatically Kate asked Frances to do the menu card for the second tearoom, the Red Lion. We do not know who designed its interior — but could she have completed her patronage to the Four, now all rather on their uppers, by giving the job to Herbert McNair? Jessie King was another prominent Glasgow artist patronized by Miss Cranston at this period — she had at least four designs for menu cards from this well known illustrator between about 1910 and 1913. Local female talent was properly represented in the decorative arts section of this exhibition — for which the convener was unusually a woman. There was no separate women's section as there had been at the previous exhibitions: women's efforts were supposed to be diffused throughout the show, reflecting an increased integration of women into the working world, though in fact male domination of the significant committees was complete. This was the period when the suffragettes were making trouble, and no one wished to give them a focus for their awkward disruptiveness.

Later in 1911 Miss Cranston, continuing her role as good fairy, set Mackintosh to redesign two earlier rooms at Ingram Street. He was otherwise unemployed, and he leapt at the chance, pouring his pent-up creativity into these modest jobs. He designed first the Chinese Room, a dark exotic area for male use, panelled and divided up with lattice screens painted a strong blue, with touches of red and mirror-glass glitter, and striking black-lacquered furniture.

In the Cloister Room, which he made an enclosed, barrel-vaulted, womb-like space, strong colour was used again in strings of rippling decoration on the warm waxed wooden panelling. The room was full of undulation. The effect was strange and novel, and like the other recent designs for Miss Cranston, strikingly undomestic. Mackintosh was using these precious opportunities to play out his current Vienna-influenced ideas. And it shows how crucial was Kate's role for him, enabling this exercise of the creativity within him.

But after this things went downhill for Mackintosh. Even Kate seemed unable to come up with anything else for him to do. He struggled on, drinking, depressed, and feeling professionally victimised.

7

'Everybody knows Miss Cranston'

At the time of the 1911 exhibition Miss Cranston was already sixty-two, but she struck everyone as being still in her prime, such was the vigour of her bearing. You could not miss her on the streets as she went on her daily rounds to oversee the smooth running of her business: bolt upright, brisk, unmistakable in her idiosyncratic Victorian 'costumes', smartly tailored to her stout figure. Her eccentric dress style softened but did not change as the years went on. She often put people in mind of Queen Victoria, but this was perhaps as much a response to her character as to her distinctive garb. She was small and imperious, and there was probably some part of her that did identify with the monarch. But there was nothing of the air of slumped glumness which had hung about the fat old queen in her last years. Kate's queenliness was expressed in a zest for doing, and an expectation of having her own way that commanded respect, though it doubtless made her quite difficult to be close to.

Nearing retirement age she was being recognised as a significant Glasgow personality. *Who's Who in Glasgow 1909* included her as one of only seven women out of 461 entries (her brother did not feature, nor her husband). Of these seven women, five were philanthropists (four of them titled) and one a factory inspector. As a business woman she was unique. That is not to say that there were not other business women in Glasgow — many services depended upon them — but in running businesses they were often hidden behind men, usually fathers or

Miss Cranston in her later years, another portrait by Annan.

husbands. Miss Cranston had made her name herself, kept it, and broken through a significant barrier against career women by sheer force of personality and unstoppable individuality.

In another very significant gesture of recognition the *Bailie* marked Miss Cranston's prominence at the exhibition with the accolade of its 'Men You Know' profile slot in July 1911, never easy of access to women. 'Everybody knows Miss Cranston', it began. 'Her name is a household word in Glasgow and the West of Scotland; her renown has spread far and wide; the BAILIE, along with all who know her wonderful business career, is proud of her and her achievements.' The magazine's eloquent tribute shows how she had by now effectively usurped her brother's claim to fame as originator of the tearoom phenomenon:

> Gifted with original ideas, business capacity, and courage, Miss CRANSTON early saw the possibilities of the tea-room if carried out on fresh and original lines, and straightway struck on a new path, along which have trooped, in due course, hosts of followers, not in Glasgow only, but throughout the kingdom. Miss CRANSTON has, of course, been marvellously successful. Everyone knows that. Why? Because of her gifts of organisation, management, taste, originality, hard work, and perseverance, and her great shrewdness in judging as to what people want. She has created a demand by the supply of just the right thing, in just the right way, and at just the right price.

She is credited with having introduced a 'veritable revolution' in catering, in which 'temperance, comfort, elegance, and economy are allied in a fine progressive form'.

Miss Cranston maintained her success by attention to detail on every front. She was known as a demanding but fair employer, and she cared for the welfare of her staff in the paternalistic and rather domineering fashion characteristic of the period in which she grew up. This comes through in what we hear from a precious witness whose memories were collected for the *Glasgow Herald* by Alison Downie. In 1909, at the age of 15, Rose Anne Quin joined the staff at Buchanan Street, the headquarters of Miss Cranston's empire, and still considered its showplace despite the glittery Willow. She worked there for eight years, rising from 'runner' (a general errand girl) to cook. She recalls an operation run with almost military precision. The girls were called 'maids' according to their work — 'potato maids, vegetable maids, pudding maids, sweet maids, stew maids'. Standards of hygiene were rigorous: the icehouse where meat was kept was scrubbed out every day and whitewashed on a Friday. Waste was frowned upon, and scraps from joints were made into rissoles and suchlike. Miss Cranston maintained a keen-eyed personal supervision through her daily visits, though the branches were run by carefully selected and trained manageresses.

The girls she took on were usually orphans or from one-parent families. Another source says that she visited the homes of prospective employees, presumably to check on the cleanliness and respectability of their background. The passing-out test for a girl in training as a waitress was to wait on Miss Cranston and Major Cochrane. Kate ran a compulsory insurance scheme for the girls — they paid in a penny a week and could draw out a guinea if they needed to go to the doctor. As Rose Anne Quin remembered, the hours were long, and the pay low (she started at four shillings a week), 'but we got three good meals every day, and though it was hard work, we were happy. It was like a big family.' This was often seen as the attraction of working in the tearooms for a good employer — it beat the isolation and often exploitation of domestic service, which had traditionally been the other main option for girls of this sort.

Altogether, as another employee remembered, Miss Cranston came across as 'very business-like — a proper business woman'. It is hard to get behind this part of her, and we know rather little of her private life. She worked so hard and identified herself so much with her business that she had less private life than most women anyway. Even her comfortable home Hous'hill was run as a productive estate. Its large gardens were not for pleasure only but produced fresh vegetables and flowers for the tearooms, and there was a dairy too, which processed milk from a field of Cranston cows. The outside staff alone numbered six around 1911 — a coachman, a stable boy, three gardeners and an apprentice gardener.

Work was central to the Cochranes' lives. The normal routine was remembered for the *Glasgow Herald* by Robert Grier, who was the stable lad, at 10 shillings a week, between 1911 and 1913. He would harness the horses, Britannia and Brutus, to the brougham to drop off Mr Cochrane in Barrhead and leave Mrs Cochrane to catch the train from Pollokshaws (the first motor car apparently appeared in Barrhead in 1905, but as we have seen, this kind of progressiveness did not tempt the Cochranes). He met her again at 6.30 in the evening. His other important task was to drive the little green donkey cart into Glasgow twice a week with produce for the restaurants. He had a smart working uniform rather like a chauffeur's.

At home in Barrhead Miss Cranston was Mrs Cochrane, and had a role to play as wife, though she can never have played it absolutely conventionally. As members of Barrhead's aristocracy the Cochranes had many social obligations, intensified during John Cochrane's spell as Provost between 1902 and 1907. They were active members of one of the minority churches at the time, the Evangelical Union Congregational Church, and had the social conscience which went with prominence and prosperity at this period, leading to support for various charitable concerns. They enjoyed concerts locally and in Glasgow: a general liking for music was marked in the Cranston family, and was strong in Glasgow as a whole at this time. They also liked the theatre: the Glasgow Rep was active between 1909 and 1914 bringing a great range of serious productions to Glasgow.

In Glasgow an important fixture in Kate's private life remained her long-standing friendship with her cousin, Mary Cranston Mason. Since the death of her father, Bailie Robert Cranston, in 1892, Mary had been largely responsible, with her brother, for the running of the chain of Waverley temperance hotels under a trust set up by his will. She also managed her own hotel on Sauchiehall Street, renamed the Waverley since the sale of the earlier Glasgow Waverley which had been run by her mother. Mary blossomed further in her fifties after the death of her husband George in 1901, when she entered public life by serving on the School Board, the main area of political activity that was open to women (the Council was not).

The Mary Mason described by her grandson Hal Stewart in the family biographical notes obviously had much in common with Kate, apart from the business acumen that made her independently more wealthy than her husband. 'She was a most kindly person, but she would stand no nonsense and had in the schools, which she visited frequently, a reputation of being rather formidable as she would not tolerate slackness either on the part of teachers or pupils.' This sounds very like Kate touring her tearooms. Mary had a lively mind, and was very well-informed. She was a great theatre-goer and maintained an active social life centred on her famed Sunday afternoon tea parties for family and a wide circle of friends, at which Kate and her husband were habitual visitors. Mary's grandchildren supplied another generation for the childless Cochranes to interest themselves in at second hand. It is from these earlier Edwardian years that Hal Stewart, who was born in 1899, remembers Kate as she was in her prime: 'dark, petite, and graceful, with a ready wit and a happy smile'. Despite her more formidable side she evidently had affection to give.

At home she lavished this affection upon her dogs (Dandie Dinmonts and dachshunds). She was also very attached to the donkey, Peggy, which drew the little green cart into Glasgow, loaded with vegetables and flowers, as was recollected by Robert Grier: '"Has Peggy had her dinner?" she would ask me, and she always had sugar lumps to give the beast.' She was also concerned, it must be said, that the lad should get his hot dinner, which he customarily ate at the Argyle Street tearooms. On one occasion it was not ready and he was about to leave when his employer discovered the situation: 'Get the boy's dinner — IMMEDIATELY!' Her caring side was characteristically somewhat forcefully expressed.

The softer side of her nature might have been expressed too in the collection of dolls she had made over the years, some of them from abroad, and beautifully dressed. These were on display in the Buchanan Street tearooms, and were much admired, particularly by foreign visitors, apparently; and she kept them after retirement. Perhaps this was another respect in which she modelled herself, maybe unconsciously, on Queen Victoria, whose childhood collection of carefully dressed dolls became known to a fascinated public in 1894 through Frances Lowe's book *Queen Victoria's Dolls*.

Kate's own artistic inclinations were perhaps expressed most directly in her love of flowers. She liked to arrange them herself, at home and in the tearooms: 'she did it beautifully', as Mary Newbery Sturrock remembered. Even Mackintosh, who apparently had a fit when Mrs Blackie put yellow flowers in her hall at the Hill House, would trust Miss Cranston to do the flowers.

So Kate lived through Glasgow's Edwardian years, working hard and increasingly prosperous. By 1913 she owned both the Willow building and the one in Argyle Street, which she had earlier rented, as well as her Buchanan Street premises. Despite many competitors in business, she effortlessly maintained her hold on the public's respect and affections.

The coming of war in 1914 brought the end of an era, though this was not clear at the time. For Glasgow it meant a boom in its heavy industries which masked the underlying decay in the economy, and after the first shock of readjustment 'business as usual' meant no decline in the use of the tearooms. There was indeed a sharpened appetite for enjoyment: it was during the war that Glasgow opened its one hundredth cinema. Nevertheless as the conflict dragged on and rationing and restrictions were introduced, voluntary at first but later compulsory, the day-to-day running of the business became fraught with petty regulations, as can be seen from a menu of that date. A full afternoon tea with crumpets, muffins and decorated cakes became an outlawed pleasure under the Cake and Pastry Order of April 1917. For tearoom proprietors it was hard to maintain standards in the face of shortages and declining quality of

NOTICE.

Public Meals Order, 1917.

On and after this date no Meals will be served in this Luncheon Room, the charges for which, as per Tariff Card, exceeds 1/3, exclusive of the usual charges for beverages, such as Tea, Coffee, Milk, &c.

Cakes and Pastry Order, 1917.

Between the hours of 3 and 6, in the afternoon, the maximum amount allowed to be spent on a Plain Tea is 6d., but High Teas including Meat, Fish, Eggs, &c., are served as usual, as per Tariff Cards on tables.

TEA ROOM PRICES.

Plain Tea, Coffee, Cocoa, Small Cup	2½d
,, ,, ,, Large Cup	3½d
Chocolate per Small Cup	3½d
Extra Hot Water (per person)	1d
Clear Soup ,,	3d
Aerated Waters, Large	3d
Small Hot or Cold Milk	2½d
Small Glass Buttermilk	1d
Bread or Scone and Butter	1½d
Cakes, French or Plain	1½d
Hot Toasted Scone and Butter	2d
Slice of Toast	2d
Cheddar or Dunlop Cheese	3d
Jam or Marmalade	1½d
Ham Sandwiches	2d & 4d
Hot Mutton Pie	4d
Scrambled or Poached Eggs on Toast	8d
Small ,,	5d
Scrambled Egg and Cheese	7d
Welsh Rarebit	5d
Buck ,,	8d

HIGH TEAS from 3 till 7-30.

FIXED PRICE HIGH TEAS

. . .

PRICE 1/3	Ham and Egg or Filleted Fish 3 Breads Varied Pot of Tea	

. . .

PRICE 1/6	Ham and Eggs or Filleted Fish & Chips 3 Breads Varied Pot of Tea	

A LA CARTE HIGH TEAS

Cold Tay Salmon & Salad	1/1
Mayonnaise of Salmon & Salad	1/1
Fried Cod Steak	11d.
Aberdeen Haddock	11d.
Fried Haddock	11d.
" Whiting	10d.
Baked Fish Custard	9d.
Kippered Herring	5d.
Potted do.	5d.
Fried Bacon & Eggs 8d. &	1/–
" " & Sausages	1/–
" Sausages & Eggs	1/–
Wiltshire Bacon & Poached Eggs	1/–
Chicken & Ham Rissole & Sauce	9d.
Fried Turkey Egg	6d.
Small Cold Roast Lamb	10d.
" " Beef	10d.
" " Tongue	10d.
" " do. & Ham	10d.
" " Round of Beef	10d.
Cup of Tea (small)	2½d.
" " (large)	3½d.
Pot of Tea (newly infused) per person	4d.
Slice of Toast	2d.
Buttered Bread or Scone	1½d.
Cakes Various	1½d.
Preserves	1½d.

SNACK TEAS from 3 till 7-30.

Fried Split Haddock	11d.
" Whiting	10d.
Small Fish Cake	5d.
Kippered Herring	5d.
Small Potted do.	3½d.
Ham & Egg	8d.
Sausage & Bacon	8d.
Boiled Country Egg	4d.
Hot Mutton Pie	4d.
Small Cold Veal Pie & Salad	4d.
Potted Meat & do.	4½d.
Cold Roast Beef & do.	10d.
Honey Vanilla Ice	5d.

For HIGH TEAS and LUNCHEONS, see SEPARATE MENUS.

Menu card for Miss Cranston's tearooms from 1917, headed with reference to wartime restrictions on consumption.

supplies — the lack of sugar especially was a sore trial to Glasgow's bakers — added to the difficulty of keeping staff. The tearooms of course had always relied heavily on female workers, but there were now plenty of other opportunities for women, undreamed of before the war, and better paid. Thousands went onto the trams and into Glasgow's factories and engineering shops, and did a great job too.

For someone with a strong commitment to quality it was a trying time, and Miss Cranston was getting old. Her brother Stuart, aged 67, retired as managing director of his business, which was ailing somewhat, in 1915. Property prices were falling and the future was uncertain. For whatever reason, Kate took the step of selling her Buchanan Street premises in July 1916 — perhaps to pay off the mortgage debt she still had on it, which must have been expensive to service — though the tearooms did not close immediately.

However it looks as if almost as soon as she had raised some spare cash the old itch returned: later that year she embarked on her last expansion. Her pleasure in new projects and in being able perhaps to bring something more out of Mackintosh seems more evident than any desperate need for more room. She was burrowing into a most unlikely space, the basement of the building adjoining the Willow: not inappropriately perhaps, and in reference to the Great War, it was to be called the Dug-Out.

Mackintosh's architectural career in Glasgow had broken down completely in a mess of drink and depression in 1913 and in the middle of the following year, after the dissolution of his partnership with Honeyman and Keppie, he and Margaret had left to go on holiday in the Newberys' favourite haunt, Walberswick in Suffolk, just before the outbreak of the war. Here they decided to stay for almost a year until the bizarre circumstance of Mackintosh, with his artistic connections in Germany and Austria and habit of solitary walks, being taken for a spy and ordered to leave. They settled in London, feeling hurt by Glasgow, and finding it easier to rub along in the artistic community in Chelsea. Miss Cranston is likely to have known from mutual contacts if not directly from them that work was difficult to come by — architectural and design jobs were scarce in wartime, and the Mackintoshes, living mainly on textile designing, were always short of money.

So hearing from Miss Cranston in 1916 must have been especially welcome, following as it did on a job for a promising new patron, W J Bassett Lowke of Northampton, which was currently underway. Kate's commission offered Mackintosh another chance to explore the vibrant geometric style — jagged triangles and strong colours on a black background — with which he had attacked Bassett-Lowke's unassuming terrace house in Northampton. It was terribly important for a work-starved designer to be allowed to turn ideas into reality — for which of course someone has to pay. This was Kate Cranston coming through one last time. She got something different and new: black walls and ceiling with stripes and chevrons in primary colours, furniture including a powerful yellow lattice-back sofa with purple upholstery, the colour and boldness a harbinger of the jazz age.

The plans were submitted to Glasgow's Dean of Guild in December 1916 and the work went ahead the following year. A memorial fireplace bore sober witness to portentous times: 'This room was opened by Miss Cranston in the year 1917 during the Great European War between the Allied Nations and the Central Powers'. It was well-intentioned perhaps, but the snazzy elegance of this 'Dug-out' might well have turned the stomach of those on leave from the stinking mud of the trenches in France — another of the myriad signs that those at home, complaining about restrictions on how much they could spend on cakes between 3 and 6 pm, still had very little conception of the ghastly reality of the war, a war which would change things more than anyone comprehended.

The opening of the Dug-Out was a last flamboyant gesture. It coincided with private disaster for Kate. A few short weeks after the work was finished, at the beginning of October, her husband became ill. A lump had formed in his throat underneath his tongue. By 9 October it was serious enough for his lawyer to come to Hous'hill to draw up a will, a simple document which left a small bequest to his brother William, and half of the residue to his wife, two sixths to Archibald and one sixth to his sister, and was mainly concerned with the repayment of £5000 which he had borrowed from Kate to put into his business. His condition grew worse. He was moved to a nursing home in Glasgow, where in the early hours of 22 October 1917 he died. It was the fiftieth anniversary to the day of Kate's mother's death. She was devastated.

8

Back in George Square

Hous'hill seemed appallingly empty without her husband, the day's routine destroyed. Impossible to return on the train to the big house, its gardens and fields, and nobody to dine with and talk about business. The heart went out of her. She was anyway 68 and contemplating retirement. Kate fled from Hous'hill and the Barrhead life back to Glasgow, back indeed to George Square where she had grown up. She established herself in the North British Railway Hotel, the only hotel remaining in the square, overlooking the sites of the three hotels where she had been born and grown up. Hotel life suited Miss Cranston, once she had things arranged to her satisfaction, and had made it clear to the staff what was expected. There was a comfort in the comings and goings, and in the sense of being back home in the heart of Glasgow, close to her tearooms. What had been perhaps to begin with a temporary move became permanent, and Hous'hill was eventually let.

However, she was withdrawing from her business. Buchanan Street, once her headquarters, which had already been sold, ceased to run as tearooms and became the Overseas Club in 1918, and was then stripped to become a bank. Next to go was the building where she had begun so long ago. In May 1918 appeared an announcement in the *Bailie*.

> Miss Cranston begs to intimate that, having sold her Argyle Street property to her Tenants, Messrs. Manfield & Sons, she will, after

Saturday 18th May current, no longer have the pleasure of welcoming the Public to her branch at 114 Argyle St. She gratefully acknowledges the long-continued support extended to her and bespeaks a transfer of her Customers' patronage to her branches at 205 Ingram St and at 217 Sauchiehall St, at both of which she has recently completed commodious Extensions, and which shall in future have her undivided attention.

But in 1919 — and she was after all seventy years old — Miss Cranston gave up her business interests completely. The Willow was sold to John Smith, a leading Glasgow restaurateur, and was rechristened in metropolitan mode 'The Kensington'; later, in 1927, it was sold on to the adjacent department store, Daly's, and was knocked through to become part of its premises.

The Ingram Street tearooms, where the property was still leased, were the only ones to run on in the old way, still known as 'Miss Cranston's Tea Rooms'. They had been taken over with Miss Cranston's blessing and help by Miss Jessie Drummond, the senior manageress who had once overseen the Buchanan Street headquarters. So these rooms ran on, a bit battered but much loved and under the old régime, very close to George Square.

Kate Cranston was remembered from this period by Jessie Drummond's niece Suzanne Boullet (her mother, Jessie's sister, married the son of Jules Boullet, a Breton who had run luxurious tearooms at Charing Cross from 1894 to 1914). She recalled for the *Glasgow Herald* a grand old lady accustomed still to command, treating her old manageress rather as a daughter — '"Jessie", she'd say, "We're going to the theatre tonight." And my aunt just HAD to go!' Miss Cranston liked to travel, and took Jessie at least once as her companion, on a trip to Venice. Most memories of Miss Cranston seem to capture vividly her forceful tone. Suzanne Boullet recalled an organ recital in Glasgow cathedral in aid of charity, and her aunt murmuring to Miss Cranston 'They'll expect you to put £5 in the plate.' The reply was 'crisp and clearly audible': 'Jessie, I'll put what I like in the plate!'

Kate's brother Stuart had died at the age of 73 on 17 October 1921. He had retired as managing director of Cranston's Tea Rooms Ltd back in 1915, handing over to his long-time right-hand man Robert Cairns. In the following year the company had jumped on the cinema bandwagon and opened 'Cranston's de Luxe Picture House', combined with extensive tearooms, after major rebuilding of its Renfield Street premises. This was a bold piece of entrepreneurialism, but restructuring in the company and wartime difficulties seem to have taken their toll, and Stuart Cranston left at his death an estate valued at a comparatively modest £3234 6s 5d for the support of his wife and the ultimate inheritance of his spinster daughter, Sybil Grace de Lace Cranston, who was apparently still living at home with her parents at 21 York Drive, Hyndland. We do not know how much brother and sister had been seeing of each other over the last years, though Kate evidently felt some bond with her niece, Sybil, who was later to come into a rather more valuable inheritance from her aunt.

Kate still went frequently to Glasgow's West End to spend time with her cousin Mary Mason, who continued her active life as matriarch. Her daughters were all clustered around her in substantial houses in the comfortable upper-middle-class residential streets of leafy Dowanhill. Mary Mason lived in the early twenties on Victoria Circus at the top of the hill, then moved to Elmslea on Observatory Road. Her oldest daughter Elizabeth and her son-in-law Ralph Robertson Stewart, a chartered accountant, lived in Athole Gardens; her second daughter Agnes and her husband Charles Mackinlay were in Dowanhill Gardens; Mary, now widowed, lived in Hyndland Road; and Elliot, the youngest daughter, unmarried, in Belhaven Terrace. To the regular Sunday tea parties came assorted family, friends and connections, some well-known, like the Lloyd Georges and Dean Inge, the ubiquitous 'Gloomy Dean' of St Paul's. Tyrone Guthrie was a regular at this period when he was producing the Scottish National Players, one of the semi-professional groups which kept serious theatre flourishing in Glasgow after the demise of the Rep in 1914. Elliot Mason was a notable actress (though amateur only while her mother lived).

Kate Cranston was grey these days but still frequently to be seen on the streets. She struck some now as 'an unhappy ghost', her fancy dress all black after the death of her husband, in another echo of Queen Victoria. She seemed more and more out of place, just as Mackintosh's interiors at Ingram Street began to seem curiously old-fashioned, as the machine sleekness of Art Deco swept through restaurant design. A new breed of tearoom entrepreneurs came to the fore, led by the big family bakeries which were now running ample tearooms, often with several branches:

City Bakeries, Craig's, Peacock's, Hubbard's. Although the growth of 'super tearooms' alongside the 'super cinemas', and the hectic postwar gaiety of much of the twenties threw a glossy cloak over the economic situation, Glasgow had begun the slide into depression early in the decade. With its industrial base outmoded and failing to counter the competition the city became the focus of Scotland's economic decline. Unemployment was a dreadful shadow hanging over its working people, and unrest on 'Red Clydeside' stoked a fear of violent revolutionary change. When severe depression came in 1929 the city was in no shape to ride it. The charitable giving of such as Kate Cranston was more than ever necessary then — she was particularly involved with the Corporation's Child Welfare Scheme which provided clothing for needy mothers and small children.

Middle-class life continued comfortably enough in material terms, but plagued by anxieties about the future. Even the tearooms were changing. In 1930 Jessie Drummond retired and Cooper's, a business founded in the same year as Stuart Cranston's, took over Miss Cranston's Ingram Street Tea Rooms. They promised to retain the character of these 'far-famed tea rooms' but it was another ending. The people who had created the tearooms were disappearing too. Miss Cranston was doubtless no longer in touch with Mackintosh: he died in London of cancer of the tongue on 10 December 1928. Margaret Macdonald lived on for four years, shifting about France and England, until she came back to London and died on 7 January 1933. George Walton, who had also been living in straitened circumstances, died at the end of that year, on 10 December 1933. In many quarters there was a sense of despondency, of the withering of old hopes.

Meanwhile Glasgow collapsed further into depression: its shipbuilding output in 1932 was at its lowest since 1860, in 1933 even lower. Well-known yards were closing, along with coalmines and factories. The streets of the old shipbuilding areas along the Clyde were quiet and full of loitering sun-tanned men, skilled workers with nothing to do.

In the early thirties Kate Cranston's characteristic eccentricity became definitely alarming. Her cousin Mary's grandson, John Mackinlay, remembered from these days her moustache and her capacity for making outrageous remarks which left a stunned silence around them. She had always been used to speaking her mind, but now her mental acuity was being undermined by dementia, and she became frightening to her young relations. This was a sad fate for such a definite person, but perhaps she was at least partly oblivious to the way her world was breaking down: Mary Mason, her close friend for so many decades, died on 11 January 1932.

We can guess at distressing scenes at the North British Railway Hotel, other guests discomfited by this strange unquellable lady dressed in black ruffles. Eventually a discreet insistence from the management that their prominent and long-established guest, who must always have been a handful, goodness knows, now needed to find more appropriate accommodation?

Steps were taken finally to relinquish the lease of Hous'hill and sell up its remaining contents. The Mackintosh furniture was auctioned off by Edmiston's at knock-down prices on 13 May 1933 — apparently only two buyers at the sale knew what the furniture was. Miss Cranston — Mrs Cochrane — was moved to a capacious red sandstone tenement, 34 Terregles Avenue, in Pollokshields, on Glasgow's genteel South Side, not far from where the widow of her cousin George lived, in Melville Street — perhaps this was what brought her to the area. Here, overlooking the railway line which might have reminded her pleasantly of the daily commuting of her business heyday, Kate Cranston lived for the last year of her life, looked after by a lady companion, Jane Fletcher. To senile decay was added a failing heart. She died on 8 April 1934, not far off her eighty-fifth birthday. After the funeral she was buried in Neilston Cemetery, Barrhead, alongside her beloved husband.

Her obituaries roused pangs of affection and nostalgia, for her figure was imprinted on countless memories just as the *Glasgow Herald* evoked her: this 'charming old lady, who in her prime and long past the age normally regarded as such was a striking figure on our city streets, as she walked briskly along, attired in quaint early Victorian costume, and carrying herself with a wonderful air.' In these uncertain times she was mourned for what she recalled for people — their youth, prosperous times, the qualities of élan and confidence which Glasgow seemed now to have lost, long sunny days before the war. This was focused in the obituaries on memories of her role at those wonderful exhibitions of 1901 and 1911, seen as the height of her achievement.

She was credited with starting the 'coffee habit' for men by keeping her establishments open after breakfast, and the 'tearoom habit' too, giving unescorted women somewhere to have a meal in public. She was certainly remembered for the beneficial social influence of her enterprise: 'In founding her tearooms Miss Cranston did more real temperance reform work than many others who devoted their life to the temperance movement' said the *Evening Citizen*. Her lively character was affectionately recalled: according to the *Glasgow Herald* she was 'a keen organiser and a model employer. She was a kindly lady with a sense of humour'.

Her role in encouraging the careers of George Walton and Charles Rennie Mackintosh was properly memorialised: she was 'the first to perceive and employ the genius of two distinguished Scottish architectural artists' (*Glasgow Herald*). The *Evening Citizen* summed up well the nature of their work for her: 'attention was given to even the smallest detail. Taste and originality were shown in the decoration, and chairs, tables, cutlery and china were all planned to harmonise with the general artistic effect.' She was seen as making a break with the stuffy past: her 'love of beauty in form and colour were a complete breakaway from the Victorian influence', a remark which returns us to the conundrum of her dress.

All in all the contribution of this 'Tearoom Pioneer' to the quality of life of her beloved city was gratefully remembered. In short, as another paper opined, perhaps floating a suggestion, 'Glasgow has put up statues to much less deserving members of the community'. A little later James Craig Annan expressed the widespread sense of loss round her passing when he wrote simply in 1938: 'Personalities like the late Kate Cranston are few and far between these days.'

She had outlived two of her executors, including her cousin William Marr, but those remaining took charge of a very substantial estate. She turned out to have been sitting on an enormous portfolio of shares, and was worth even in these depressed times, a staggering £67,476, twenty times more than her brother Stuart when he died in 1921. Bequests included £100 to Mary Sharp, 'formerly one of my assistants in business' — she had been the 'sewing maid' who kept uniforms in repair and also made the costumes for Miss Cranston's beloved dolls; and £200 to Thomas Erskine, a baker, also an employee. Her favourite brother-in-law Archibald and his daughters, Isabel and Jean, received £500 each, as did Ralph Robertson Stewart, Mary Mason's son-in-law, a chartered accountant who was in demand as an executor in the family, and Elliot Mason, still unmarried, for whose actressy independence Kate had always had a soft spot. There were substantial bequests to two favourite charities: £4000 each to the Saltcoats Mission Coast Home and the Saltcoats Child Welfare Homes.

Her brother Stuart's daughter, Sybil Grace de Lace Cranston, also still unmarried, was considerably enriched by her aunt: she received her four pear-shaped diamonds 'mounted for hair-pins' and all other personal articles apart from her diamond engagement ring, which went to her husband's sister, Marion McLean, and her diamond brooch and her two single-stone diamond ear-rings, left to her husband's nieces. Sybil also inherited a third of the residue of this large estate. As for the remaining two thirds: 'I desire this to be applied for the benefit of the poor of the city of Glasgow'. So, fittingly, it was in the end the people of the city she loved who profited most from Kate Cranston's lifelong business acuity.

Epilogue

'That wonderful woman appeared to have in view her own aesthetic gratification more than the rapid accumulation of a fortune on conventional restaurant lines', commented Neil Munro in his autobiography. But such was Kate Cranston's acumen and force of personality that she both pleased herself and made a fortune. In short she got away with it: she achieved an unusual degree of freedom, expressed outwardly by dressing as she wished, and an unusual degree of success (she died richer than all the other main characters in this story), all within the period when women were still deemed incapable of voting responsibly.

Towards the end of his life, in 1927, Charles Rennie Mackintosh wrote, rather loftily: 'Our ideal is to work for the best type of individual and the crowd will follow'. Miss Cranston had been this 'best type of individual' par excellence, and had done an enormous service for a difficult talent. Mackintosh was well known for uncompromising behaviour as an architect: at least he could compromise, but not happily. It looks as if Miss Cranston never seriously asked him to, but allowed him something close to a free hand. This was a precious gift, enabling, particularly towards the end, a stylistic development which might otherwise have been frustrated: for the trouble with being an architect and interior designer is that someone has to pay if the work is to be realised. Miss Cranston was happy to pay, and evidently this commitment paid her back, not only in cash, but in the reputation she craved. Her patronage of Mackintosh, which was a natural progression from her patronage of George Walton, enabled the expression of that personal need to be extreme and different which carried her through life.

Now that Mackintosh receives posthumously the wide acknowledgement he was denied when he was working, Miss Cranston's reputation is carried by his. The rediscovery and admiration, indeed adulation, of Mackintosh has been bound up in the last quarter of the twentieth century with Glasgow's revitalisation and rebirth, a process in which design and the expansion of service industries have played an essential part. The beginnings of this reconstruction can be traced to the 1970s, a century after Miss Cranston's small beginnings in Argyle Street in 1878. Biographies too easily compress time, and it might help expand our sense of the length of Miss Cranston's career and the change it witnessed if we try transposing it like this to our own time, relating it to our own lived experience.

On this timescale she first employed George Walton in 1988, the year when Glasgow's Garden Festival, a century after its first great exhibition, expressed this sense of the city presenting a newly confident face to the world. The first job that Mackintosh did for Miss Cranston at Buchanan Street in 1896–7 is shadowed a century later by the enormous impression made by the Mackintosh exhibition shown in Glasgow and the United States in 1996–7, with the restored interiors of the Ingram Street tearooms as its centrepiece. Following this time-line in our imagination, the revamping of Argyle Street coincides with Glasgow's year as City of Architecture in 1999, the Ingram Street ladies' lunch room will be unveiled in millennium year. Ahead in the new century lie first the next international exhibition in 2001, then the Willow in 2003, and in 2004 Miss Cranston's new house. There is a trailing off of commissions between 2005 and 2011, when there is another flurry for an exhibition year. Then nothing until 2016–17, which will see Mackintosh's last job for Miss Cranston, and her husband's death, followed by her retirement, approximately forty years after she began. Her own death will not occur until 2034.

It was a long career, a lot of hard work, the building of a special enterprise, particularly in a decade round the turn of the century, which contributed something very distinctive to the city. Neil Munro's contemporary, the humorist J J Bell, catches this nicely in his autobiography: 'I am reminded of the Londoner whom I took into Miss Cranston's first tea room. He sat down at the dainty appetising table, and exclaimed "Good Lord!" — as well he might, poor devil, being used to nothing better than the cold marble slabs and the canny methods of his London A.B.C. shops.' Miss Cranston herself cannily had shares in the Aerated Bread Company — and J Lyons & Co come to that — but what she had traded on was something individual, stamped with an excellence stemming from the way that the tearooms expressed her personal fulfilment.

She was not like anyone else. She made a significant impact on the lives of her fellow citizens, not by good works, but by meeting their needs and expanding their horizons. Many observers attested the individuality and energy of her city at this period, a vitality and flaring, smoky splendour that persisted alongside its close-packed squalor. As the journalist H V Morton wrote in 1929: 'There is nothing half-hearted about Glasgow. It could not be any other city.' Miss Cranston, her own creation, personified the panache of Glasgow in its heyday: hence the affection and esteem in which she was held by the inhabitants of that great city.

INDEX

SELECT BIBLIOGRAPHY

Burkhauser, J, ed, *Glasgow Girls* (Canongate 1990)

Crawford, Alan, *Charles Rennie Mackintosh* (Thames & Hudson 1995)

Kaplan, Wendy, ed, *Charles Rennie Mackintosh* (Glasgow Museums/Abbeville Press 1996) with full Mackintosh bibliography

Kinchin, Perilla, *Tea and Taste: The Glasgow Tea Rooms, 1875–1975* (White Cockade Publishing 1991, 2nd edn 1996)

Kinchin, Perilla, *Taking Tea with Mackintosh: The Story of Miss Cranston's Tea Rooms* (Pomegranate 1998)

Kinchin, Perilla and Juliet Kinchin, with a contribution by Neil Baxter, *Glasgow's Great Exhibitions: 1888, 1901, 1911, 1938, 1988* (White Cockade Publishing 1988)

Moffat, Alistair, *Remembering Charles Rennie Mackintosh: an Illustrated Biography* (Colin Baxter Photography 1989)

Moon, Karen, *George Walton: Designer and Architect* (White Cockade Publishing 1993)

Oakley, Charles, *'The Second City'* (Blackie 1946, 4th edn 1990)

Stewart, Hal D, Biographical notes on various members of the Cranston family, in the possession of Dr C J Mackinlay

Quoted in the text

Downie, Alison, 'Kate Cranston by those who knew her', *Glasgow Herald* 13 June 1981, p 9

Lutyens, Edwin, *The Letters of Edwin Lutyens to his Wife Lady Emily*, ed C Percy and J Ridley (Harper Collins 1985)

'Muir, J. H.', (= James Bone, Archibald Hamilton Charteris and Muirhead Bone), *Glasgow in 1901* (William Hodge 1901)

Munro, Neil, 'Erchie in an art tea-room', originally published under the name of Hugh Foulis in *The Evening News*; republished in *Para Handy and Other Tales* (Edinburgh 1931). Available now in Neil Munro, *Erchie & Jimmy Swan*, ed. Brian Osborne and Ronald Armstrong (Birlinn 1993) pp. 100–4

Munro, Neil, *The Brave Days* (Edinburgh 1931) p 199

White, Gleeson, 'Some Glasgow designers and their work', part I, *Studio*, 11 (1897) pp 86–100